W9-CEY-951

Conversations
with
God the Father

Conversations
with God
THE FATHER

Encounters
with the One True God

Mark R. Littleton

STARBURST PUBLISHERS
Lancaster, Pennsylvania

To schedule Author appearances write: Author Appearances, Starburst Promotions, P.O. Box 4123 Lancaster, Pennsylvania 17604 or call (717) 293-0939

Website: www.starburstpublishers.com

CREDITS:
Cover design by Terry Dugan Design
Text design and composition by John Reinhardt Book Design

We, the Publisher and Authors, declare that to the best of our knowledge all material (quoted or not) contained herein is accurate, and we shall not be held liable for the same.

Conversations With God the Father
Copyright ©1998 by Mark R. Littleton
All rights reserved

This book may not be used or reproduced in any manner, in whole or in part, stored in a retrieval system or transmitted in any form by any means, electronic, mechanical, photocopy, recording, or otherwise, without written permission of the publisher, except as provided by USA copyright law.

First Printing, April 1998

ISBN: 0-914984-19-5
Library of Congress Catalog Number 97-80891
Printed in the United States of America

DEDICATED TO:

The members of Westbridge Church, Des Moines, Iowa. The dream church I never thought I'd find. Thanks for giving me the chance of a lifetime.

Contents

Introduction

All my Christian life I've had questions. Questions like . . .

Why don't they come right out and say "Jesus is God" in the New Testament?
What's going to happen in the future?
How can I be sure I'm going to heaven?
Would God ever change His mind about loving me and my family?
How come Jesus lived when He did? Was there some strategy to that?
Why didn't He live at a time when the whole world could easily know about Him and His miracles?
Why has God let the world get so messed up?

And so many more. If I could just get a couple of hours with God, face to face, and ask Him all these things, so much would be straightened out.

Well, here's my (and your) chance. Granted, these interviews are imagined. I don't claim that they are directly from the mouth of God, or that they're inspired, or anything like that, *as some books claim*. They're strictly a result of my own imagination, creativity and understanding of the nature of life.

However, having known God since the summer of 1972 and

having had a multitude of conversations with Him in prayer and in my head since then, I think I have some good ideas about what He might say about some of my questions.

I know what you're saying: What makes me an authority? Nothing, except that I've known Him for 26 years and that's certainly enough time to develop some informed opinions about Him. I don't pretend that these conversations come from anything but my own personal understanding of God. But I think you will find it a uniquely fascinating understanding, as many people have told me who have heard me speak and who have read my books.

But please understand, I don't claim to have any more authority than the next guy who knows the Lord personally. Perhaps I've learned some things others haven't. Perhaps I have something to say about God that others haven't said. I hope so. Nonetheless, be assured they are from the heart and soul of a person who loves God and who wants others to know Him as well as He can be known.

In fact, that has been the prayer of my life for many years. "Lord, I want to know You as much as You can be known—like Paul, and Moses, and Abraham, and Peter did."

I think as you read, you will find a personality on the page that is irresistible. If God is who I think He is, He is the most beautiful Person who has ever existed. That is what I hope to accomplish: to get that beauty on paper so that many people can learn of Him and love Him the way His most committed disciples have throughout history.

If you're like me, you have a lot of questions about God that have never been answered satisfactorily. Maybe when you read this book, you will find a few answers that not only satisfy, but which energize, inspire, challenge, and edify.

If so, then this book will be worth the struggle.

Why Did God Create Us In The First Place?

People all through history have asked this question. Perhaps a story will answer it. This is a story about an imagined conversation between me and God on the day He decided to create earth. Perhaps you'll find some intriguing insights within, at least I hope so. But as you read consider: God created all of us for reasons known only to Himself. No matter what your position or place in life, God has given you things that make it worthwhile. It's that outlook that I hope you'll tap into as you read.

A Fantastic Decision

I've thought about it for years, but only recently did I begin to grasp it. I'd like to say it all came in a flash, or a dream, even a vision. But frankly, I'm not sure He would communicate it that way.

Just the same, the experience changed me. Or should I say the insight.

The issue is Creation. You, me, all of us from all time. Angels, demons, amoebas, giraffes, houseflies, skunks, the whole shootin' match as some say. What concerned me was not just Creation. It was why. Why He took the trouble. Why He did it, knowing what would happen—evil and its consequences.

That is, unless He didn't happen to know that evil would wreck everything. But of course I can't believe that. He's omniscient. He knows everything that is, was, and will be. Every possibility.

It's stupendous.

But I'm getting away from the issue.

I imagined myself going to Him. To the throne room I mean. A sort of adviser. I imagined that we were there at the beginning, before anything was, before He'd even begun the first act of Creation.

He told me about this plan to create a multitude of angels—very majestic creatures, marvelous to watch, fascinating.

I said, "You know, Lord, that if You create these angels, one of them will rebel and lead a third of them in a war against You."

He nodded and told me He realized that.

I asked, "Why create them, then, if they're going to cause so much trouble?"

He told me we were getting ahead of things. He said that after the rebellion of these angels, He would create a whole universe and another set of beings called humans (of which I was one). They would be even more incredible than these angels because they would be "in His image," reflections of His character and nature. Only they would be on a lower scale since they'd be more confined—fixed in time and space.

Of course, by now I was upset. You see, I knew precisely what would happen: the second rebellion. I began to shake. He asked me what was wrong.

I said, "Lord, don't You know that shortly after You create the first humans they also will rebel against You, turn Your world into a place of havoc and despair, revile You to Your face, and hate You?"

He nodded and for the first time His face whitened.

I shuddered. I thought He might weep. But He composed Himself and told me He knew all that would happen.

I couldn't restrain myself. I cried, "Lord, You can't create them like that. You'll have to make it impossible for them to rebel. It'll only be pain, forever and ever. Your own heart will be crushed within You. Please stop this before it goes too far."

He gazed at me and took a breath. I waited quietly. He didn't speak for a terribly long time. Finally, He said, "Do you suggest I create an inferior being then, one without My sacred mark upon it, one without the fullness of My image?"

For the first time I felt uncomfortable. I said, "Perhaps You'll only dispense with the test then in the garden, the freedom to choose good over evil. Maybe if they weren't tested, it would work out."

He replied that was impossible, for that was what made them most like Him.

I said nothing, but my heart despaired.

He then told me of His other plans—how He would redeem the humans through a series of steps, culminating in a sacrifice which He Himself would make.

Of course, I knew instantly what He referred to. I said, "Lord, You're speaking of the suffering and death of Your Son, Your only Son, who is as much a part of Your being as the human heart is of His."

He nodded and closed His eyes. For the first time a tear glinted His eye.

This was too much for me. I said, "Lord, You are aware that your Son will die on a cross, the most torturous form of execution these rebellious humans will devise in their hatred of You. You know they will hate Him, curse Him through the ages. The few who do believe in Him will also be driven from the planet like rats from a beach. You know that in the moment He dies He will be separated from You and suffer a pain greater than all the anguish and agony of all of hell's inhabitants combined."

I was angry. But as I gazed at Him, His whole body shook, and suddenly great heaves racked through Him. I knew now how it hurt Him even to think of this, His Son's suffering. I felt a great compassion for Him. I said quietly, "Lord, You do not have to take this step. Nothing has yet been created. At the risk of even me not existing, I have to say to You that the cost and the pain are too great."

He was looking at me, penetrating me to the heart.

I continued, "Lord, there's still time. You can make some other world, some other universe, one that will do only as You desire."

He continued looking at me, kindly, understanding. Finally, He said, "Such a world, as we already discussed, would be useless to anyone."

I cried, "Then don't create it at all, Lord. Give up this dream. There's no point."

He shook His head. "No," He said, "there is something you have forgotten."

I waited.

"If I don't create such a world, I will never do the very thing for which I am who I am—a creator. A creator must create. It is his nature."

I thought about this. "But You are also love, and grace, and goodness, and justice. What about these?"

"Even these are useless characteristics unless they have some way of manifesting themselves."

I thought hard. I believed He was not yet given to this. Before I could speak, He said, "You have forgotten something else."

I waited. It seemed that His great form trembled. "Is not fellowship important?" He asked. "Isn't what you have in Me important to you? Do you not think that the price of My own personal pain is worth the value of love, friendship, and a kinship of souls?"

"Yes, for us," I admitted. "But You don't need it, Lord. You can exist without it."

He smiled. "Of course. But what if I don't want to?"

I swallowed. I was astonished. This was getting more difficult than I had imagined.

"When you were down there building your house, was it worth the creation of the house to smash your thumb a few times?"

I looked down. "I suppose."

He seemed to be looking far off. A great tear fell from His eye, but He didn't speak and I waited a long time, saying nothing myself. Partly for fear. Partly for reverence. And partly, yes, partly— no, mainly—because this was what I had come for. This was the revelation I had longed to understand.

"There is something else," He said. "If I create, there will be much pain for all concerned. But I will make a way for all to find redemption and hope in the midst of their pain. In making that redemption, I will pay an ultimate price, a price which even I shrink from paying."

I nodded. That was precisely the reason I wanted Him not to do it.

"But," He said, "does a brave man shrink from doing what is right and best even if it costs him his very life?"

He looked at me, the eyes gentle, pained, but kind and joyous inside.

I couldn't speak.

He smiled, the shy, brave smile of a person who must give all in order that another might live.

He said, "This is something I want to do, this sacrifice."

"Just to do it?" I said, suddenly confused. It seemed almost self-satisfying.

"No," He said with a wistful look. "No, not just to satisfy Myself. That would be pure selfishness. No, I want to do it because . . ."

I waited again. I gazed deeply into His eyes. Somehow there I saw all the centuries of angelic and human battles against Him. I saw the arrows of hatred piercing His heart. I could feel the swords of rejection and malice cutting great gashes in His soul. I could see all the faces of those who had rejected Him, their voices rising up in accusation against Him.

The horror was so great I flinched and turned away.

But something drew me back.

I looked again, and this time I saw something deeper. I saw the Son rising. I saw Him triumphant. I saw Him defeating all those enemies beneath His heel and turning, embracing those who loved Him. I could see them kissing Him and holding Him like children who thought all was lost and now have discovered it has only just begun.

I saw His kingdom, too glorious to fathom. I saw the Son reigning, the Father above it all, both revelling in the joy of Their creations who, now, having turned from sin and perdition, have come to know Their love in all its varieties.

I saw the legions singing, climbing, ruling the world and Creation with perfect justice and righteousness. Never again a cheat. Never again a murder. Never again a loss, or a forced entry, a broken bone, or a firing squad to dispatch a hundred lives at the flick of a trigger.

I saw them drawing near Him, basking in His transcendent beauty and light.

And then I saw myself. My family. My daughter, her cheeks rosy, her face shining as I read to her The Great Story. My son, tossing a ball to me and screaming, "Strike one! It was a strike! Right, Dad, right?"

Grandfather teaching me to carve. Grandmom baking me a cake. Mother taking me out to buy my first suit. Dad showing me how to tie a bowline.

My people. The heritage of long lasting thousands.

Then I saw us, He and I, walking, talking, joking, laughing, running together, racing, climbing the mountains of His holiness together. I saw Him and me, sharing a rose, inspecting the petals, revelling in the beauty. I saw Him and me, traveling the galaxies, watching the light refract through the jewels of His kingdom and coming away, choked up in the crush of it all. I saw both of us standing among lions, galloping together on stallions white as snow, and flying on the wings of eagles.

I saw us, our hearts knit together in such a love that no sword, no deception, no demon, no rain of hail or darkness of night could dispel it.

I was almost too stunned to speak. My heart seemed so full I thought it would burst.

But then I saw one thing more: Him. His heart. Suddenly, I saw the very marrow of His soul, the glory of His character. I saw the depth and height and length and breadth of that love and grace that would sacrifice all—His very life and blood—that I might live. I saw how He transformed me from an idler to an eternal wonder, from a horror to an honor among all Creation, from mere man to the image of Himself.

And I saw myself reigning with Him forever and ever. A prince. A king. A man after His own heart. One for whom He died.

"Do you understand?" He said quietly.

I nodded, my throat too constricted to speak.

Suddenly, I loved Him with an intensity I had never before known. With joy, I bowed in worship before Him and sang the songs of Zion.

As joy surged through me again, I wept and looked into His face. I said, "Lord, I want to be like You in every way. Make me like You. Teach me to love as You love."

He said quietly, "I will."

At that moment, I fell into His arms, overcome.

And then a moment later, found myself here. In my bedroom, on this warm, soft cushion. My wife next to me. My children in the next room. I closed my eyes and wept.

As I said at the start, I can't be sure everything here is correct. It was only an insight, a musing. But I had to tell you. For His sake. Because He is worthy. Because He is far greater than I ever imagined.

This story gets at the heart of what I'm trying to say in this book. God is worthy: to be known, to be loved, to be worshiped. It's my hope as you read these pages that you will find the Personality of all personalities, the King of kings and Lord of lords, the One who loves us and who desires that we love Him in return. If, at the end of this book, you find yourself saying, "Yes, I want to know Him," then I'll have accomplished what I've hoped to do.

The Conversations

First Things

So here we are.

Indeed.

What am I supposed to say? You're great, You're tremendous, I love You, something like that?

You can say anything you want.

And You can say anything You want.

Then that puts us on an even footing.

So . . . I'm not sure I know what to say.

Then say nothing.

I can do that?

Of course. Why not? Why wouldn't it be that way? I never get bored. I would never tune you out. I have no need to attend to other duties. I'm here for you. So say and do what you want. I'm always here and prepared to listen.

Always?

Always.

Why?

(He laughs.) It's complicated. Let's just say that's how I am, what I do.

Doesn't it ever get dull?

Never.

How come?

Because when people talk to me, usually they're alone, they're sincere, and they're in trouble. So they don't beat around the banana tree.

Banana tree?

My variation.

So You have a sense of humor?

Could the One who created the platypus, giraffe, and you not?

I suppose. I never thought You'd be this way.

What way did you think I'd be?

You know—holy, powerful, doesn't take nothin' offa no one. That kind of thing.

Well, I am those things—to some degree. But perhaps not as you've imagined.

Undoubtedly not. I'm sure I have many misconceptions.

Indeed you do.

(I feel miffed.) You needn't get nasty about it.

Nasty? Was that nasty?

No, but I didn't think You'd be so blunt.

You thought I'd beat around the broomstick some?

Yeah.

Then what do you think I should say? Should I lie to you? Should I embellish it? Should I overlook it?

No, I guess I'd appreciate Your being completely honest.

Then we're thinking alike. Because that is what I do best.

You're not going to hurt me, are You?

Not unnecessarily. But any relationship involves pain, hurt, rejection, misunderstanding. I anticipate we'll have those emotions and experiences in our relationship. But that doesn't mean I would inflict pain just for fun, or because I'm angry, or because I'm jealous or something like that. A surgeon inflicts pain to heal. I think of Myself that way sometimes.

As a surgeon?

A healer.

Yes, I can see that.

Good.

(I think about that response.) Why are You always so . . . so . . .

Nurturing?

Sort of. Positive is the word I was thinking of. Encouraging is better.

I like to encourage people.

Why?

Because encouragement is good, helpful, uplifting, balming. I want to make our time together friendly but reverent. I don't want you to feel insulted, rejected, bored, or backed into a corner. Or worse, condemned. I don't operate that way. And for that reason, I try to be encouraging and positive. But I can confront, too. Or rebuke when necessary. Don't try to put Me into a slot. It'll make things harder.

It will?

Of course.

Why?

Because then when I find it necessary to speak with you about hard things, you will find I can be very direct and blunt and even uncompromising and that may throw you off. You may feel that I'm more than you bargained for.

What happens then?

We go on, and get it worked out.

You won't make me eat my shorts?

(He chuckles.) No.

You won't cast me aside?

No.

You won't file for divorce.

No.

So even when it's rough, it's good.

That is My desire.

Okay, well, I have to go.

Fine, I'll be here when you need Me, or want Me, or even when you don't.

Thanks.

Have a holy day.

A what?

My variation.

Sounds horrible.

It's not.

Well, see You.

Indeed.

God On God

WHO HE IS, WHAT IS HE LIKE?

God Is Love

I've heard that You are love. Love itself. Does that mean You're an emotion?

Love is not an emotion.

It's not?

Love is two things: it's a person, Me, and it's a way of coming at life, an attitude, an outlook that leads to right, true, and holy action.

All right, I've heard this before: "God is love." How can You be love? It's like the Force in Star Wars. There, God, or whatever the directors meant, is called the Force. It's both good and evil. It has a good side and an evil side. You plug into whichever side You're on, and then it does things for You.

Like?

Like lift rocks and rocketships.

I can do that.

Don't be funny.

Aren't the things the Force does rather trivial? Certainly nothing worthy of the true nature of a God who created the universe. What exactly does the Force do? The biggest thing is to help Luke Skywalker at the end of the *Star Wars* movie to fire the torpedo into the right hole. He listens to his feelings to do this. How nebulous is that? Feelings change constantly. Those who listen to their feelings for every decision they make will end up becoming terrifically confused. This Force idea works in the context of a movie. But in real life it's just more impossible Hollywood mumbo-jumbo.

So You've seen Star Wars?

Many times.

(I laugh.) Why?

I'm omniscient. I know everything that is, was, will be and could be. I saw *Star Wars* before George Lucas was born. Before the universe was born.

Hmmm.

The point is that I am love in a way that has nothing to do with the concept of the Force. I am love in that everything I do is characterized by love. I am motivated by love. I am purposed by love. I act in love—always. And I choose to do the loving thing—in all circumstances.

Then why do things go wrong?

The moment you add a second and third and fourth person to the equation, things get complicated. If they're not acting out of love, then other factors impinge on the situation. Like human freedom.

So Your love can be thwarted?

In a limited way, yes. In an ultimate way, no.

But You're God. Can't You do anything You want?

I can only do what My character allows Me to do. I cannot sin. I cannot do evil. I cannot act without considering holiness, righteousness, goodness, truth and love, to name a few of the attributes that motivate My decisions. I can do anything I want to do, but what I want will be governed by the intrinsic qualities of love, holiness, and so on. What you're really asking is, can I do anything you dream up and think I should do?

I guess that's what it comes down to.

Like, will I bail you out of a bad situation which results from bad decisions that you and others have made?

Wouldn't that be the loving thing to do?

Not necessarily. Letting people live with the consequences of their bad decisions helps them to learn to make good decisions in the future. That's the essence of wisdom, the very wisdom I'm trying to build into the lives of My people all over the world. Love and wisdom tell Me that simply bailing a person out of a tight spot is not the best thing to do. Thus, while you think I should do it as an act of love, I'm seeing the greater act of love in letting you suffer the consequences.

But why? What's the point? Some of us are really hurting down here?

And I still do bail people out. Many times. Consider Lourdes. Do you think all those supposed miracles are untrue? No, I work in and through people all the time. And I do miracles in the world constantly. But not every time. In fact, I rarely do miracles today simply to lift someone out of a tough spot. Instead, I choose the wiser course of inducing growth and maturity over a simple act of power.

Let Me give you an example. Mother Teresa was regarded the world over as a saint, as a great woman, as the kind of person who is truly godly and godlike. I agree that she has done wonderful things for multitudes of people. What she did was nurse people who were ill or dying. She found them in the gutters of Calcutta and gave them dignity by providing them a bed and a place to die among friends and people who loved them. Many of these folks had no one their whole lives. Mother Teresa stepped in and loved them unconditionally. No matter how rank their sores, no matter how disgusting their illness, she tended them, touched them, wiped their brow with her kerchief and wept real tears over their passing. Is Mother Teresa not a miracle, and people like her the real miracle? Rather than healing those people supernaturally, I sent them My love in the form of a person who could care for and console them. Which would have been better, to heal physically through divine intervention, or to heal emotionally and spiritually through divinely-inspired human love? Sometimes I do one, sometimes the other. But I choose the latter more frequently than the former. Why? Because that kind of love benefits hundreds of people, perhaps millions, including Mother Teresa herself. A miracle is just a quick fix. It will last only till the next illness. Love lasts forever.

But so many people suffer.

Yes, but you're seeing it from an earthly perspective. I see these people as eternal creatures who will populate an eternal heaven. Their suffering next to eternity is just a moment of time. It's better to suffer a little now and grow through the pain, than bring a person to heaven who expects a miracle a minute. It's foolishness.

Suffer a little?

Have you ever read what Paul said about it in Romans?

Probably.

"I consider that the sufferings of this present time are not worthy to compare to the glory to be revealed." When you consider all that I have planned in the future, nothing anyone goes through now is of much consequence. Only as it enables them to become mature, godly and holy people fit for eternal habitations does it have value. Paul was right. Even beheading, which happened to him, meant little in the long run. What is fifty years, or seventy, or a hundred, next to eternity? Of course, I sympathize and empathize with people who are suffering, and I stay with them, listening, helping, strengthening them the whole way through. Do you think I don't know their pain intimately? I know every tremor My people experience. I hear every cry. It cuts My heart to hear My children in pain.

I'll tell you about a young man I know. He was a police officer, a good one. He often counseled people he was called to help. He gave them loans, his own money in times of need. He visited people he knew were lonely. The day of his death he had stopped by a lady's house just to comfort her in her distress over an abusive husband. He was in a classic sense a good man. He was also severely depressed. Afflicted with a biochemically-caused mental and spiritual depression, he tried every cure his doctors could think of. Nothing worked. The darkness and agony inside his mind would destroy a lesser man in a month. But he hung on for over three years, seeking healing, praying, doing his job, loving his wife and children, and caring for his loved ones. I loved him like a son. The pain, though, reached a crescendo in that last year and it wouldn't stop. In the end, he shot himself in the head in his bathtub because he didn't want to create too great a mess for his family to clean up. He loved them to the end, and I wept over his pain and his death. The whole town he worked in turned out for his funeral. He will be sorely missed. He is with Me now, and Jesus' comfort has released him from his agony. One day, his whole family and many of those he loved will join him in heaven and their reunion will be joy to My heart. But for now, his wife and children suffer with the grief of his departure, and many good people accuse Me and wonder why I didn't heal him. It would have been such a simple thing. But if I were to explain to you all the reasons and causes for his death from My point of view as the sovereign Lord who had complete charge over the situation, you would not accept them. No answer I give to this world will satisfy you or anyone else. You will only raise more questions and find more problems with each level of the explanation and our argument will go on, if possible, until the day you die. For that reason, I never try to give such answers. I can only assure you that when you arrive here, in this eternal place where your mind and your heart will possess complete perfection and total spiritual comprehension, then and only then can I give the kind of answer that will make sense. As great as that policeman's pain was at the time of his suicide, even he sees it as a small thing compared to the glory he experiences now. It comes down to a single question: Will you trust Me with everything—your pain, your fear, your worry, your past, your present, your future—everything? Because if you will, I assure you that you shall know the truth and the truth shall set you free.

That's what Jesus said.

And what I say too. Such trust is why a perspective of life that takes the long view is so essential to survival in this world.

The Long View?

Seeing things from the perspective of eternity, as I see them.

I'm not sure what you mean.

Take Job. Here was a man who suffered. But the period that he suffered and lost so much was a matter of a few months. In the end, I restored double to him of everything. When you get beyond suffering, when you're whole again—either in this world or the next—it never looks as bad as it did when you were in the midst of it. Take the long view and you will see that no matter how difficult it is now, later will make up for it. A hundred times over.

What does this have to do with You being love?

You're asking the questions here.

All right, but if You always act in accordance with love, how can You send people to hell?

> I don't send anyone to hell. People and angels choose hell, quite consciously, by rejecting Me over and over throughout their lives. I come to them, implore them, beseech them, beg them to believe in My Son, appeal to them to stop sinning and start following Jesus, and what do they do? They laugh in My face. In the end, they choose to live in a place which is utterly bereft of Me and all I am and do. That's hell. It's a place of torment because they experience all the emotions and pain of longing for the things they can't find there.
>
> Think of it this way. Suppose you're thirsty. What do you do? You get a drink of water. I have provided water (or Coke, iced tea, whatever).

Which do You prefer—Coke or Pepsi?

> They taste the same to Me.

You and everyone else! Except a few weird people.

> Yes, I know the feeling.
>
> What I'm saying is that when you're thirsty, I've provided a means to allay thirst. You drink something and the thirst goes away. Well, what if you're in a world where you have rejected Me and all of My work (Creation, water, life, happiness, food, etc.) how can you satisfy that thirst? You can't. So it just gets bigger and bigger, more overwhelming, more overpowering. Soon you're burning up with thirst because you're in a place where there's no such thing as water.

Or Coke.

Right. So what happens? You burn. You're feverish. You're crazed with thirst. And then something else happens: you become hungry. You dream of a Big Mac or a Whopper— I've tasted both, don't ask Me which I prefer, My people are in both corporations—but there's no Big Mac or Whopper anywhere to be seen, because you're in a place where they don't exist. So you just get hungrier and hungrier and soon you're burning up on that front. Added to your thirst is hunger. What happens? You burn with desire. Add to these all the other realities of life (the desire for sex, sleep, shelter, hope, love, kindness) you can't get any of it in hell, because you're in a place where I am not. You're where you have chosen to go because basically you've said to Me, "I want nothing to do with you. Leave me alone." That's hell.

Sounds awful.

It is awful. And I long and desire that no one go there.

You really do?

Of course. Why would I wish hell on someone I knit in the womb, someone I loved all their lives, someone I wanted to be part of My kingdom? No, I don't want anyone to go to hell. But they do, because they choose it over Me and My Son.

So You love them even though You have condemned them to hell?

Yes, I love them. But remember again, I did not condemn them to hell. They condemned themselves by their own choices.

But maybe if You'd warned them or something?

I warned them many times. In each life, once they reach an age where they must account for their choices, I give them multitudes of warnings: through their conscience, by speaking in their hearts, by the warnings of other people. Every time they had a friend die, every time they passed a graveyard and a church, every time they were tempted, I warned them not to continue in their hatred and rejection of Me. But in each case, they made a real and conscious decision to go their own way.

You play for keeps.

Absolutely. This thing called life is serious business. You can't approach it with a lackadaisical attitude as if you will never be called to account for what you do with it. Every person will stand before Me and answer for what he or she did with his or her life.

But all of us have made mistakes.

Yes, and that was why I sent Jesus. He died a horrid, agonizing death in the place of each person who has ever lived, from those who died in the womb, to those who died at the age of Methuselah. When a person believes in Him, he never has to worry about paying for his sins and mistakes. He never need worry that I will ever bring up a single wrongdoing. Jesus paid for it all.

That's why You want us to believe in Him?

Yes. He is the way to life, hope, and eternal bliss in heaven.

The only way?

Has anyone else in human history died for the sins of mankind?

I guess that answers my question.

I'm sure we'll come back to it.

Well, we certainly covered a lot this time.

I don't give easy answers. But I think they're easy to understand.

They make sense, when You look at them in the light of day.

Okay, let Me rest. I'll be back. Hasta Luego.

Finding Me

Father, why do so many people in the world not know You? I know people all over who have all sorts of ideas about You that from what You've said so far makes me think they can't possibly know what You're like. Some hate You. Some just want to avoid You. Many don't want You interfering in their lives. If knowing You is so great, why do so many want nothing to do with You?

It's one of the hazards of being God.

That people don't like You?

I have enemies that tell loud lies against Me. Unfortunately, many people believe the lies rather than hear Me out. For instance, what's one of the main things people say about My Word, the Bible?

That it's full of contradictions.

Correct. But can they name one? Rarely. In fact, the reason they say that is because they heard some teacher or prof or friend or relative say it—without backing it up—

and they use it as an excuse not to find out who I am through My Word. It's a boldfaced lie. The Bible was written over a 1600 year period by over forty authors. Some languished in prison. Some were kings. A few were prophets. A select few were executed because of what they wrote. The amazing thing is that these authors agree on a multitude of controversial issues that have plagued mankind since the beginning of time. Now if you were to take ten authors from the same time and same circumstances and you were to compare what they wrote on just one controversial issue, how much agreement would you find?

You'd probably have ten different opinions with a vast range of ideas of what they called truth.

Definitely. My Word is an amazingly concise and complete book. It speaks of Me and I am ultimately its author. That's why it speaks with such unanimity on so many difficult issues. But people still say it's full of contradictions. Why? Look, I'll tell you a story to illustrate it.

Four beggars sat around a fire sharing jokes and stories. One of them spoke of an enchanted forest. He said, "A prince lives there who gives fine gifts and a royal welcome to all who visit."

The other three were interested. But they asked, "Then why haven't you gone to his house?"

The first one shrugged. "We all do what we want to do."

Though the other three were skeptical, they decided to find out for themselves. They set off in search of the enchanted woods. After a journey of many days, they came to a strange forest where birds sang and sat on your finger, beavers gave firewood to travelers, and the chipmunks brought nuts and berries to every stranger. The beggars made a fire and settled down for the night.

After all were asleep, the second beggar awoke at a sudden noise and noticed a light through the trees. He got up and soon discovered it was a great house. He knocked on the door and an ancient man greeted him, inviting him in. The beggar expected to find great treasures within. But instead, there was nothing but a large table with a loaf of bread upon it.

He asked the ancient man, "Where are the treasures?"

"Here," he said, pointing to the bread, "the greatest treasure of all, the bread of heaven."

The beggar snorted and headed for the door. On his way out of the forest, he wakened the third beggar and told him he was heading home, the whole thing was a hoax.

The third beggar decided to see for himself. At the house, he was greeted similarly and the ancient one showed him the bread.

The beggar inspected it closely and decided it might sell in the nearby town. He took ten loaves with him. On the way out of the forest, he roused the fourth beggar and said, "Look, there's not much treasure here, but if you hurry up the bread looks like it might sell in town. I've got ten loaves. You can get your own."

The fourth beggar went to the house. When the ancient one showed him the bread, he was instantly pleased. The ancient one gave him a piece. As he ate, it seemed that his mind and heart filled with good things he'd never known before. "This is marvelous bread," he said. "I've never had anything like it."

"There is nothing like it," said the ancient one.

As they talked, it seemed that the fourth beggar's eyes began seeing things he'd never seen in the house before.

Suddenly he jumped up, "Why it's a treasure chest full of gold!" He ran across the room where a huge chest over-flowed with gold.

"Yes," said the ancient one. "Take as much as you like."

The fourth beggar shivered with amazement. "I don't need much, so long as I'm here with you. I won't take any till it's time to leave."

"That's wise," said the ancient one with a nod.

They sat down together by the fire and shared their stories. In no time, the fourth beggar came to enjoy the ancient one's friendship. But then he noticed a huge pool of water on the other side of the room. "What's that?" he said jumping up.

"Living water," said the ancient one.

"For drinking or bathing?"

"Both. And more."

"Please, I could use a bath," he said and took off his clothing.

The water was cool and warm at the same time, and a delicious feeling of contentment came over him as he lay in it. "Do you swim in this yourself?"

"Of course," said the ancient one with a twinkle in his eye. "You certainly seem to be enjoying yourself."

As the fourth beggar looked around, he saw more trea-sures all over the room. And the room itself seemed to grow bigger. "Why it's a whole world of treasure," he said as he clambered out of the pool and toweled himself off.

"Yes," said the ancient one. "And you haven't seen the first hundredth of it."

They sat down together by the fire and shared their stories. In no time, the beggar came to enjoy the ancient one's friendship, and he stayed many days. But one day the fourth beggar decided to head back for town and tell others about the house in the woods.

When he reached town there was much disagreement for, he saw his friends and began inviting people to come dine on the bread of life. The second beggar told people it was nothing but lousy loaves of bread. The third beggar screamed about him interfering with his business. People joined with each beggar and soon there were many different groups in town shouting about the others being charlatans and liars.

Nonetheless, the fourth beggar ignored their taunts and continued to invite people to come taste the bread of life in the house in the forest. Many people came, and ate the bread and partook of the treasures. But the beggar especially enjoyed the ancient one himself and his stories about the king. It seemed he learned every one of them by heart.

Then one day the ancient one approached the beggar, saying, "I must go on a long journey. Will you take care of the house? It's not mine, as you know, but the King's. All you must do is receive travelers, offer them the bread and treasures, and take care of things."

The beggar was overjoyed. But he said, "I'm only a beggar. How can this be?"

The ancient one laughed. "You're no longer a beggar, my son. You're the new master of the enchanted wood. It's all yours until the King Himself returns."

The beggar trembled and was silent a long time. "I never thought anything like this could happen to me."

The ancient one smiled. "Anything can happen to him who believes and obeys. I also was once a beggar like you."

But the beggar didn't even show surprise. Somehow he knew it was the truth, almost as though he'd known it all along.

He watched the ancient one walk off down the road, then began preparing the bread for whatever travelers might come. "They'll have it just like I did," he said and sat in the main room, waiting, eager for the first guest to arrive.

Good story. I liked it.

Yes, but what does it illustrate? It shows how different people look at Me.

The first type, like the first beggar, heard something about My house, but he wasn't interested. It would take too much effort. A second type of person, like the second beggar, is eager to find out what heaven has to offer, but when he discovers it, he's disappointed. He runs off in a huff. The third kind of person, like the third beggar in the story, recognizes that the things of God have value, but only insofar as they can provide a way to get what the world offers. Thus, some people become religious because of the prestige or position it gives them in the community. Or it becomes a way to do business. They never taste the true bread I offer.

The fourth beggar in the story was the only real seeker. He hungered for the bread of heaven and discovered it only by humbling himself and tasting it. Then he went out to invite others to share the treasure.

I can see that.

There's more. While the bread of life satisfied the fourth beggar, the others didn't even taste it. This demonstrates that not everyone seeks the true bread of life, though everyone is hungry.

Hmmm.

There's something else. All four beggars responded differently after their encounter with the bread. When you're offered such a gift, you must respond. Indifference, attack, manipulation are all responses. The one who tasted the bread, though, was transformed and began to reach out to others.

Jesus often spoke of this idea when He told His disciples what kinds of responses He'd get to His work and presence. The Pharisees attacked him mercilessly. Some people tried to use Him for their own ends, like Herod. Others were indifferent, like many of the scribes.

He also made it clear that anyone who wanted to find God and faith would have to become a beggar. Jesus said, "Unless you are converted and become like children, you shall not enter the kingdom of heaven." He meant that only when we come to God like a child coming to his father—needy, dependent, humble, open—can we begin to see what life is all about.

Powerful story.

I'm glad you liked it. That reminds Me of one other truth about this story: when the fourth beggar ate of the bread, his eyes were opened—gradually. He began to see the true treasures in God's house. That's the way it is for anyone who seeks Me. Their eyes are opened at once, but their vision only clears gradually. They see Me as Father, but they don't see everything. It's those who endure, who learn and who grow, who grasp the full breadth of the treasure I offer. But it also shows why so many refuse to come to Me: their motives are skewed, their hearts are wrong.

But You can change the heart.

> Yes, but I cannot wrench a heart away from itself. I must work hard and long to woo a heart from the old life. It takes much effort.

But it's worth it.

> Of course.

Can I share this story with other people?

> You can share any of My stories with others.

Good. It helps me understand things.

> That's why Jesus told stories—to help people understand. I put within the heart of mankind a love for stories. It's the way of life as I created it.

So how does a person find You?

> By seeking Me with all his or her heart.

And they shall find You?

> Absolutely. It's My most fervent promise. Anyone who seeks Me will find Me if they search for Me with all their heart.

That's in the Bible.

> Yes, I made it up.

And because You made it up, it's the truth?

> You're catching on.

I'm a quick learner.

Holy, Holy, Holy

There's a concept that I guess I find hard to reckon with: Your holiness. Several times in the Bible, You're addressed as "Holy, Holy, Holy," and it's the only part of Your character that is ever spoken of that way. We don't say, "Love, Love, Love," or "Peace, Peace, Peace." It seems that holiness is an exceptional quality that You must be very proud of.

Proud?

Maybe that's the wrong term. It's a quality that You want us to know is extremely important.

It is the one quality that sets Me off as utterly unique in all of Creation. Partly because I am not part of Creation; and partly because Creation does not possess holiness in the same way or form.

I think of holiness as austere, stern, religious, sacred. I think of it like we humans think of nuns, or monks, or priests, or pastors. They're these people who live above it all, who don't get their hands and lives dirty, who rarely crack a smile and who are always sober, straight, and sharp.

Another S might be serene.

Serene?

Holiness is serene. To be at peace with oneself because you know who you are, what matters, what you want to do and where you're going. Holiness is, above all, a condition in which there is no trouble within oneself.

No guilt?

Yes.

No worry?

Yes.

No fear?

Yes.

Why?

To be holy means being reserved for only the best in oneself. For instance, your mother served special dinners on her one-of-a-kind closeted china. She brought it out only on the most important occasions. It was reserved for the finest meals, the most decorative occasions.

Sunday dinner.

Correct.

Entertaining close friends.

Of course.

But how is that like holiness?

Being holy means that you are always at your best, at your most truthful, generous, kindest, most loving. You never cater to low values or deeds. You always do what is right, wisest and most beneficial for all concerned. You never stoop to base actions like lying, cheating, or stealing. You always do what is right, even if it hurts you.

Pretty heady stuff.

More than that, without Me being perfectly and infinitely holy, you could never be sure I really cared about you.

Without holiness I become a loving fool, an all-powerful tyrant, an omniscient busybody. It is holiness that makes everything work together perfectly.

Like a well-oiled machine.

Only I am not a machine. I am a person. Three persons actually with one essence.

The Trinity?

Yes.

Now there's another . . .

Let's stick to the subject, shall we? Or does this make you nervous?

A bit.

Why?

If You're as holy as You're saying, if You're as perfect as it's made out to be, how can You stand the sight of us, down in the slop, killing, hating, reviling, cursing each other, complaining incessantly, taking Your name in vain, committing all sorts of sexual . . .

I think you've made your point.

Sure, but . . .

I try not to listen to too much about such things. They are repulsive to Me for the very reason you say. I am holy and am not only above and beyond such doings, but I detest them with a hatred and disgust that you can't imagine. It is My holiness that demands more of My creatures than what they normally give. It is My holiness that says to them, "Follow me, and I will make something greater and better of you than you could ever do on your own." It is My holiness that pushes Me to go after every sinner and try to stop them from sinning.

But if You can't bear the sight of us . . .

I am not only holy, but wise, loving, and gracious, among other things. Holiness makes Me hate sin. Love and grace make Me pursue the sinner to redeem him.

I think holiness must be a great deal more than that.

It is.

Well, what?

It's hard talking directly to you about these ideas. But one of the most important elements of My holiness is that I am lofty. I am exalted. I am far removed and above Creation, so far above and beyond it that no one anywhere could ever approach Me unless I choose to let him.

Whoa!

You cannot look directly at the sun in daylight. Yet that is just a created object, a ball of gas and fire. My holiness means that no one could even look at Me without being burned up immediately. No one could enter My presence without being snuffed out like a doused torch, to mix metaphors.

But . . .

My holiness means that we couldn't even have this conversation. My words and thoughts are so far beyond yours that you could never understand. My glory and greatness are such that you would shrink from even stepping into My throneroom. How would you feel if the President of the United States suddenly called you to the White House for a conference? Awed? Amazed? You probably wouldn't speak until spoken to. You would never do anything wrong in his presence for fear of the consequences.

Now imagine flying a spaceship up to the edge of the sun.

I know a joke about that.

I've heard it. But tell Me again.

It's like a Polish joke, except it's about Slobovians.

Yes, a mythical people renowned for their foolishness.

Seems that they built a spaceship they were going to fly to the sun. They were asked how they planned to do it since the sun would burn them up. They said it was really no problem, they would fly at night.

Ah, Slobovians, the milk of humanity.

Anyway, You were saying . . .

Imagine flying a spaceship up to the edge of the sun. You'd have to put on thick shields and armor to do it. But even then it would never happen. You'd be burned up long before you ever got within a million miles of it.

In a way, that's My holiness. Like the sun, I am high and exalted, glorious and powerful, and no one can look Me in the eye without turning away. No one could come near Me without being burned up. No one can see My face and live.

Then what hope have we of ever knowing You, let alone seeing You face to face?

Without My Son there is no hope. But with him, there is

total hope. He broke down the wall that separates Me from you. He ripped open the curtain that veiled the holy of holies in the Temple at Jerusalem. He makes it possible for anyone to know Me personally and fully, eyes open. Only in him is that possible. That is why He is the Way, the Truth, and the Life. He alone can impart the things that make people live in My presence with joy.

Joy?

Of course. Do you think there will be anything less than raucous joy in My throne room?

All this holiness talk makes me shiver.

It's holiness that also lets Me laugh, lets Me give pleasure to My people, allows Me to enjoy their friendship, stories, and personalities. Holiness is a wonderful truth, for it is holiness that not only scares you and silences you in your sin, but it is holiness that welcomes you into My arms when you become a believer. It is holiness that invites you to partake of the pleasures of heaven. It is holiness that lifts you up to My level, while it is sin that keeps you down and fearful on your level. Holiness exalts the person; sin degrades him. Holiness makes him true and wise and good; sin destroys all those qualities.

So it's a good thing?

The best.

But how is it possible for us to enjoy You if You detest what we are and do?

In Jesus I don't detest you, because Jesus paid for the sins of the whole world. He wiped them all away. Because of him, I can love, enjoy, and walk with you as if you'd never been anything less than perfect.

I'm not getting this.

Perhaps a story will help. I know a man named David who once had a stray dog visit his back yard. The small black dog jetted about, never pausing but always looking for food. When the dog found food by the trash, he ate it in fear, always prepared to dart away the moment David appeared. One day, David began putting food out for the dog whom they called Streak. Streak would eat the food when David went away. But when he stood there, beckoning, speaking kindly words, the dog stood far off, shivering and whimpering.

One day after many weeks of kind words and steady food, Streak decided it was all right to cower in front of David as he ate, but he never let David come near. He'd always run off if David approached.

Finally, David got an idea. He went to the dog pound and found another dog not much different from Streak, befriended him and took him home. This dog he named Edward. Eddie for short. He began feeding Eddie in the backyard and when Streak appeared, he let the two dogs become friendly. As Streak saw how Eddie responded to David, Streak grew friendlier. And one day, Streak simply leaped into David's arms. From then on he was a member of the family. Eddie had shown him the way.

In a sense, that's what Jesus did. He showed people the way to Me. Of course, he did far more than simply act as a go-between, but that's the root of it. In Jesus, we have a friend who brings us back to God the Father. He shows people I can be enjoyed and loved just like the friend I am.

It's a good illustration, because it shows Streak was afraid of You at first. That's like Your holiness. You're so far and high and exalted that we can barely cower in Your presence. But as we get to know You through Jesus, we find You're no ogre, rather a friend, one who wants to be a father to us.

Exactly. And thanks for no longer considering Me an ogre.

Well, after all this talk about holiness, I was beginning to wonder.

Just remember that My holiness insures everything else.

How so?

> Holiness insures that I will always be loving because I'm not operating on the same level as you. My holiness means I'm high and lofty, yes, but it also means nothing you do can change My regard for you. I am so far removed and above the things of this world that you cannot change Me or make Me act on a level that is below My nature. I will always treat you with love, respect, generosity, and gentleness because I am holy and I cannot be anything less than that.

Interesting.

I hope it's much more than that.

Yes, it is, but at this point, I'm a bit awed.

> That is what My holiness should produce. It's not that I want you to be awed because I'm this weak, insecure, celebrity-infatuated person who craves fame and glory. No, you should be awed because I am awe-ful, to coin a pun. I am a most amazing person. But you know what?

What?

You are a most amazing person, too. Because I made you like Me. And one day, were it not that I won't permit it, angels would worship you as God, because you will be such an amazing and awe-ful reflection of myself. I intend to make all those who believe in Me to be the true crowns of Creation. And no one will ever call you Short-stuff again.

No one calls me that.

I used to call you that.

You did?

Just kidding. Actually, it was your uncle who called you that, if you recall, but I gave him the idea.

My uncle had a nickname for everybody.

You want to know what nickname I called him?

Sure.

Rugambamahalottojambutanniscalandra.

Pretty long nickname.

Called him Jambo for short.

What's it mean?

Guy who gives everyone a stupid nickname.

That fits. Tell, me do You ever laugh?

All the time. Do you think I could possibly be omniscient and not laugh at the things I see all over My universe? People can be very funny, better than any sitcom. I laugh best when My people laugh hardest. Their jokes are My jokes. Did you know I play jokes on you?

Not really.

> All the time. The other day you were stopped by a police officer for speeding. He gave you a warning. Why? Because he saw your sticker on your bumper that said you donated money to the police fund. It was a joke.

Not a very funny one.

> But I knew you couldn't afford to pay for a ticket, and I knew you couldn't afford to speed. So I had the policeman stop you and only give you a warning. A little joke.

How so?

> What happened when you told your friends about it, the whole thing about how you donate to the police fund specifically to get that sticker? They laughed. They thought it was wonderful. I had the policeman stop you specifically to give you a chance to tell your story about the stickers. Your joke on the police. My joke on you.

I was scared.

> You were praying your boots off.

That he would just give me a warning, right?

> No, that the sticker would work.

Hmmmmm.

> The world is a lot of fun for those who will walk with Me. I make it fun and an adventure. Wouldn't you agree that your life has been an adventure?

In a lot of ways.

I made it that way. I give adventures for faith. A free exchange.

This is almost unbelievable.

A lot of things about Me are. But you know the beautiful thing about it all: they're true. No matter what My enemies will tell you, everything I've told you is the truth. And one day it will all BE.

I'll be there for it.

Hopefully we'll all be there for it.

Amen.

Truly.

Do You Understand What It's Like?

Sometimes I think You don't quite understand, Father. You're up there in heaven. You have all You need. You own everything. How can You identify with me, a middle class white guy with a regular job and bills to pay?

There's a story I love to tell about that.

Tell it.

People in a certain kingdom were angry. They said the king didn't understand. They said he didn't know what it was like to be oppressed, to be beaten, to be rejected, to be hated. They said he had no right to judge them, or ask that they obey and trust him. They said if he understood it might be different. But he could not possibly understand.

So the king decided to make an offer. "I will come

among you and be one of you," he told them. "I will become a common man."

"But you will come as a prince," they complained. "Few of us are princes and most are cruel."

"No," the king answered, "I will come as a pauper, the son of a laborer. I will work hard every day for my bread and water. I will hew in the fields. I will wield the scythe and cut my own yoke. I will have to break my own horses. No one will help me do these things. I will see what it's like to live on the land and touch the dirt and strive for every penny I earn."

"Perhaps," the people said, "but you will be a citizen, respected and protected."

"No," the king told them, "I will be an outcast. Some will spit upon me. Many will hate me. They will not love my words. They will despise my deeds. They will reject and scorn me. I will be the guy on the team who gets chosen last. I will be the fat boy who people make fun of. I will be the dumb one who can't complete his homework."

"But you will come as a healthy, happy person with a great family, who has nothing but good all his days. You will have riches and honor from your peers. You will be respected in the marketplace. Your family's name will support you. None of us have a family name, but you will have one."

"No," the king replied, "I will remain unmarried. I will have no children, no legacy, no one to call me Papa, no son to be proud of, no daughter to praise. No grandchildren to grace my lap. No loved ones to call me Relative, and Uncle, and Father. I will know little more than sorrow all my days."

Some of the people were intrigued now, but they said, "Then you will live long and well and never know great physical pain. You will be healthy and never lick a sore or bandage a wound."

The king answered, "No, I will die a criminal's death, at a young age."

There was a long silence. "If you are to do this," the people said, still skeptical, "then you must come in an age when the world is in great turmoil; you must live in a world run and controlled by ruthless people; and, above all, you must be a member of the most hated race on the face of the earth: the Jews. If you can do this, perhaps you will truly have been one of us."

"Done!" the king said. "I will fulfill all your requirements." And he did. He came among the people. He spoke quiet words of wisdom that many listened to. He performed deeds of kindness that made him loved. But he didn't have riches. He didn't have a position. He didn't have honor. The authorities constantly tried to trap him in his wise words. They worked to destroy him and complained that he was an imposter, a fake. But the king stuck on, right to the end, when he died, on a cross, on a highway of the world, where all crossroads meet, and they looked upon him and watched. Some hated and longed for him to die. Some wept, and prayed for him to live. But all were amazed at how he died.

And after he died, he rose from the dead on the third day because of his deeds and words. The whole world learned of him. And many came to believe he was the greatest king who ever lived, the only king who ever truly understood what it was to hurt and weep and cry out in pain and labor and be rejected. Many loved him so that at the end, when the king took his throne again, he made them members of his kingdom, princes and princesses and they reigned forever and ever in the style of the king who understood his people.

That's a story about Jesus.

Yes.

What He did for us.

Correct.

So You do understand, through Jesus, what it's like, for instance, to be tempted?

Yes. Every temptation you have ever faced I also have faced in Jesus. Only I never gave in.

Then You don't know what it's like to give in?

I know what it's like to want to. But if He'd had ever given in, He could never have paid for the sins of mankind. He would have had to pay for His own sins. I know the results of giving in, though. I know what it's like to feel guilty, because Jesus bore the guilt of mankind on the cross.

So You do know what it's like to give in?

Yes.

You know what it's like to wish for something so bad that You would give Your right arm to gain it?

Jesus did, in the Garden of Gethsemane. He wished that He did not have to go to the cross.

You know what it's like to hunger for understanding?

That's the story I just told. But what about the king? Do you think He ever longed that his people understand Him?

I don't know. I suppose. Do You long for understanding?

It is better to understand than to be understood, better to empathize with those who hurt than to desire empathy from others.

But don't You ever?

I am understood by those whose own understanding is infinite.

Who?

Jesus and the Spirit.

So You don't need us to understand You?

I want you to understand My heart, My love for you, My desire to help you grow and see the truth and live in grace. But I don't expect the finite to completely comprehend the infinite. That would be asking the impossible.

I thought You could do the impossible.

I can do the impossible, but I can't ask for the impossible from My people.

I understand.

Good. Then we have had a meeting of the minds, as you sometimes put it.

A meeting of the hearts, perhaps?

That, too.

I want to understand You, Father, more than anyone else in Creation.

You will. You will one day understand Me as well and as much as I can be understood by a human in My image.

That's enough, then.

Enough for Me, too.

Let's go for a walk. I'm tired of sitting.

Here, let Me rub your back.

You do that?

Best back-rubber in the universe. Besides your wife, of course.

Ahhhh.

The God Who Gives And Keeps On Giving

I've read and heard a lot about Your grace, and how gracious You are. But frankly I'm not sure I understand what it's all about.

In all My dealings with mankind, I act in grace. Since I owe no one anything, no person has a right to demand anything from Me. Thus, in order for anyone to receive something from Me, it has to come from My side, My choice. I have to choose to grant his request, or prayer, or whatever. I am under no obligation to grant it, but because I am gracious I often do.

That sounds a bit arrogant. You don't OWE anyone anything?

On the contrary, everyone OWES Me EVERYTHING.

Everything you have in this life is from Me. Food, clothing, shelter, mate, children, everything anyone possesses is ultimately from My hand. They may not know it or accept it, they may even think they've earned it somehow. An Excessively Rich Person—I'll call him ERP—may think he did. But I gave ERP his intelligence, his acumen, his business sense, his opportunities, his growth, his employees, his place in time and history. I could easily have put ERP in Jericho the day that Joshua blew his horns and the walls fell down. But I chose to put him in this century, in America, in a place where there was freedom to use his gifts. I gave him the opportunity to deal with huge corporations and to create fantastic products that become smash, bestselling hits. If it was not for Me, ERP would be no one and nothing. I could have had him grow up a Jew in Nazi Germany and then allowed him to die in the camps. He could have been born a slave in Roman times to a harsh taskmaster. I could have made a million other choices about him that would relegate him to being the poorest man on earth instead of one of the richest. But I have done what I have done. Often, ERP doesn't seem to know anything about Me, in fact spurns Me. It's grace that keeps Me from destroying him this very minute.

You sound a little bitter.

Not at all. But people don't understand this. Let Me repeat it: I don't owe ERP or anyone else anything. I give them life, a time, and a place. And I give them the sustenance to live. As Jesus put it, I make the rain to fall on the just and the unjust. I do that, because I am gracious. Because I like giving gifts to people. Because I know that without Me you couldn't exist. I do it because it's My nature to give and keep on giving, even when the one I give to hates Me, spurns Me, denigrates Me.

Why do You do it then?

Because I take responsibility for My own. I know you can do nothing apart from Me, so I'm willing to do My part, even if they're not willing to do theirs. If I so choose, I can knock down a man or woman financially, emotionally, or spiritually at will. But most of the time, I choose to build them up. I enjoy seeing people flourish and grow. I like to see them tackle problems and succeed. I like to give them a sense of meaning and accomplishment. I made you all that way, and I don't like withholding the very things I created you to crave.

But so many other people in the world have nothing. Why just the other day I was perusing a magazine and there's a picture of people slaughtered in Rwanda. Did You do that?

No. Rebels, hateful people, and murderers did that.

But why didn't You give those people what ERP has?

What ERP has will last his lifetime on earth. When he departs, he will take none of it with him. If he has not become a believer in My Son during his lifetime, it will all be for nothing, for he will be judged for his deeds in the body just like Hitler, just like Joe Schmo. I raise some up in this world, and I put some down. Most stay in the middle. These are My choices. But I make such choices for a very good reason.

Why?

That people will begin to look to Me for their needs, for

their rewards, for everything. If I made everyone like ERP, then there would be no one like ERP. In reality, the very gift of life makes every person on the same level as ERP anyway. I've just given ERP a fortune on loan. That fortune belongs to Me. I give it to whom I desire, and I withhold it from whom I desire. ERP will have it for a short time. Sure, he'll boast. Sure, he'll think he's something. But when he stands before Me, he will answer for everything he's done. And then his fortune will mean nothing. Only his true character and nature will matter then. He cannot buy his way into heaven, nor can he buy his way out of hell. His fortune is only a figment of his imagination. He thinks he has something, but if he does not have life in the Son, he has nothing. His riches are actually, in many ways, a curse. Remember what Jesus said?

The camel?

Yes. It bears repeating. It is easier for a camel to go through the eye of a needle than for a rich man to enter the kingdom of heaven. It's true. Few among My children are rich. Riches blind a person to the truth. They think because of their riches that they have accomplished something above and beyond all others. They think they have made it on their own. They think they are better, more important, more secure, superior to others. But in reality, as with everything else, they have what they have because I gave them the equipment to achieve it. Their riches may prevent them from coming to faith in Jesus, and that will be their greatest misfortune. They trusted in wealth, which is uncertain and can disappear overnight. They should have trusted in Him who could grant to them the real riches.

What are the real riches then?

I have only given you an inkling of them in My Word. A relationship, a friendship, a fellowship with Me and My Son is the first thing anyone receives who enters My kingdom. When you are related to Me, I make it My obligation to meet your needs, to be with you through trouble, to be a friend in loneliness. Do you know what it is not to fear? Not to fear trouble? Not to fear temptation? Not to fear setbacks and evil circumstances and evil people? A person who is related to Me does not need to fear anyone and anything. Who can stand up to Me? I am all-powerful. Goliath thought he could defeat Israel because he was nine-foot-nine. He heaved a heavy spear. There was no sword created like his. And yet David killed him with a sling and a single stone. Why? Because I was with David, I guided his hand, I enabled him to whirl the sling enough revolutions to insure the velocity needed to break through Goliath's skull, I assured the trajectory of that stone, and I made it strike the spot on his skull that was most likely to give way and cave in. I gave David everything he needed to defeat Goliath. All he had to do was believe and swing the sling. Few people would want to face a Goliath in mortal combat. But I am much greater than any Goliath. And I send My faithful ones to face and defeat Goliaths every day.

Remember when Sennacherib attacked Jerusalem and Hezekiah came to Me and asked for help? What happened? Sennacherib's army of 185,000 warriors was decimated in a night because I sent one of My angels to slay them. One angel. There are billions of them in Creation. And yet, I am more powerful than any angel as well as all of them put together. Like one of your poets has said, "One plus Me is a majority." It's true. Are you afraid of walking down a dark street? Take My hand. No robber can stand against Me. Are you worried your bank account will dry up? Trust Me. I own the cattle and the banks on a thousand hills.

Now You've gone to preaching.

It's an exciting subject for Me. I love it when a person wants a relationship with Me, because I know that from that time on they will experience—and I will too—something blessed and beautiful that lasts forever. Remember this: you can tell Me the secrets of your heart, the things no one else on earth knows about. I know your heart. I know what's there. Even a spouse, even a child who loves you, can never know you like I do. I know your thoughts before you think them. I know what's going on in the recesses of your soul, and I can feel deeply about what you're feeling and thinking. You can't share those things with any other person. But you can share them with Me. That is the glory of a relationship with God. We can reveal our hearts to each other on a level that is so intimate and rich you would exchange it for nothing else in this world, not wealth, honor, power, or fame. And yet, it is so simply won: just faith. All you must do is believe, and you have Me and all I am and own forever. I think that's a pretty good deal.

But it's not all one-sided, is it?

No, I get something out of it, too. I enjoy knowing you. You are a great friend to Me. I respect your thoughts and opinions. I will listen to you and not drop off to sleep, ever. I will go with you into the depths of any darkness and not complain for a moment that My knees hurt or My eyes are watering. I will live with you through the heat of the day and the cold of the night. I will take your hand in the valley of the shadow. My rod and My staff will be comfort for you in the dark alleys of life. All these things give Me great satisfaction, to do these things for you and know that you will be grateful for them.

On top of that, you're important to Me. I appreciate your friendship, your ideas, your hopes, your fears, your worship. It thrills Me more than you can imagine. Why? Because this is what I created you for. From the beginning, the only thing I have ever wanted with humanity is a fond, loving, and joyous relationship in which I can give you every good gift I can create, and you can give Me, in return, your love and worship. I get something out of it, and so do you. In fact, I get a lot of out it. Frankly, I never want to lose our friendship. If you were to stop yourself tomorrow and say, "This God stuff is bunk. I'm giving it up," I would be deeply hurt. Just as you've hurt when someone you love has rejected you, so do I. I never want to lose what we have. Never. And I will fight to keep it. That's just how I feel.

That's very humbling.

Perhaps. But I don't mean to humble you, only to be honest. I love you and that can never change.

You're going to have me bawling in a second.

Go ahead. I do sometimes. The beauty of a mutual, loving, respectful and intimate friendship is incomparable. But that's only one of the riches I have given you in grace. A second is forgiveness. Jesus accomplished that on the cross. In him, I forgive those who believe for everything they've ever done wrong, intentionally and unintentionally, past, present, and future. I wipe it all away. What did I say in My Word? That I have separated your sins from you as far as the east is from the west. That I have thrown them into the deepest sea. That I have hidden them behind My back. That I will never again look upon them. That I have blotted them out, like a cloud disappears on a sunny day. When you come to Me, I don't see the taint of sin on you anywhere. You are as pure as fresh snow. And I hold nothing against you. That means you have nothing to fear from Me. I will never punish you for anything you've done wrong, because Jesus was punished in your place. I will never blame you for any of the world's other ills, because I have blotted out your sins. They're gone. Finis. Never to be brought up again.

Have you ever seen what happens in a typical marital relationship? Many times the wife or husband will be angry about some slight. They will argue. Then one of them begins bringing out the big ammunition. They blame the other for all sorts of things. They bring up old sins, old slights, old mistakes and sling them at the other like arrows. It can destroy a relationship.

You will never have that from Me. I will never mention one of your sins ever, under any conditions. They're gone. Evaporated. Destroyed. Wiped out. Forever.

That's pretty awesome.

I'm glad you see the value of it. And that leads to a third gift I've given all My children: salvation. Salvation from sin. Salvation from themselves. Salvation from the second death. When someone becomes a follower of Jesus, his name is immediately written in the Book of Life. He becomes a member of My family. You know, sometimes I laugh when I think of British royalty. They can be so smug. But they don't have anything they weren't given. Unlike ERP, they haven't even earned what they have. They were just born into it.

Yet, the world over, how many people would love to be part of the royal family? Multitudes. If not them, then members of a rich family, or a powerful family. People crave the opportunity to become part of a rich, powerful, and revered family. They dream about it. They make wishes. You should see all the prayers I get from ladies asking Me to send them a true prince! You should see all the men who desire a princess! And yet, when you become a believer in Jesus, you are immediately made a member of the most royal family there is: Mine! If you think Buckingham Palace is something, you should see what I have prepared for My family when they get to heaven. And if you wish you had riches like ERP, believe Me there are a million success stories up here for the one who believes. ERP is little more than a tub of cheap ice cream compared to what I intend to shower on those who are My children for all eternity.

But we're getting off the subject.

You sound very enthusiastic about it all.

I am. I love giving gifts to My children. What father doesn't? I remember when Joseph gave Jesus his first tool kit. It was an august occasion. Joseph beamed. Jesus marveled. It was such a small, simple thing. But in that household, it was a gift fit to their income and status.

Well, listen to this: I give gifts to My children in proportion to My status and position, too. What did the magi give Jesus at His birth? Gold, frankincense, and myrrh. Gifts fit for a king, from kings. Kings do not give glass jewelry to their beloved. They give gold and diamonds. So imagine what I am capable of giving, I who own everything in the universe? I give My gifts in accordance to My wealth. A poor man gives a penny. A rich man might give a million dollars. But I, who have created all things and can easily double or triple them all at a word, give gifts according to what I own. And I give gifts that no one else can give: peace to the bereaved, joy to the sorrowful, hope to the despondent, kindness to the beaten down, gentleness to the abused. I give freedom and serenity and fortune and fame in proportion to My own possessions. Since they are infinite, imagine what I'm capable of to the one who will seek Me?

(I laugh.) This is blowing my mind.

Let it blow. I want it to blow. I've been wanting to tell people this for ages. What I plan to give to you and all My other children is literally out of this world!

You crack me up.

It's exciting, isn't it? But that's only the beginning. I give many other gifts that we haven't spoken of. Wisdom. Power. The right to rule. A seat at Jesus' right hand. The White Stone—have you heard of that? The Hidden Manna. An inheritance. A home in heaven. Many homes in heaven. Myself. There are a multitude of things I've revealed in scripture that I will shower on those who believe, just because they believe. Why? Because I have the power to give. I love to give, and I will not be outgiven. That's how I feel.

This is incredible.

Hang in there, you haven't seen anything yet.

I'll be back. Let me step out for a drink of water.

I'll be here, there, and everywhere.

Old Beatles' tune?

No, just an expression.

The Trinity Of Divinity

Father, one of the most confusing things about You that I have learned in the Bible and in church is that You're a trinity. But the Bible never uses the word, "Trinity," and nowhere does it talk in explicit terms about it. I'd like to know: what are You—three Gods, three persons, two persons and a spirit, what?

Not all things about Me are easily understood. I am one. When people speak of God, they speak of one God who is over all and through all and in all. However, within My God-ness are three persons: Me, My Son, and the Spirit. We are three distinct persons who have different personalities and different responsibilities. We work together, but We also relate in what some people call a chain of command. I, the Father, am the lawgiver, the ruler, the sovereign, the head, the one who is over all and in all. My Son is the King of kings and Lord of lords over humankind. He is the head of the church. He sacrificed His life on mankind's behalf. He is a servant, a son, and a sovereign in human affairs. To put it in modern business terms, He answers to Me. He must give account to Me and carry out

My orders. But He is also My equal and My greatest friend. He walked in earthly sandals and knows the feel of a human skin. He is utterly unique among us in that sense.

The Spirit answers to the Son. He inspires the Word of God. He seals believers in their faith. He opens the hearts and eyes of the lost. He, the Son, and I possess a fellowship and friendship that is unsurpassing in the history of divine affairs. All three of us created the universe. All three of us work out the process of human salvation. All three of us will appear in eternity and in final judgment.

We are one God, one in essence, in power, in deity, in camaraderie, in attribute. But We exist as three distinct persons. In trying to understand this, people have devised different ways of illustrating this truth. For instance, they say that water exists in three forms: liquid, solid, gas. But it's all H_2O. Others have used the idea of a chicken egg, which has a shell, yolk, and albumen. In a way, these examples are comical to Me—theologians's attempt to simplify the sublime. It is undoubtedly an impossible task. In My Word I have not tried to explain our three-in-oneness for that very reason, just as I have not tried very hard to explain heaven. You can't understand them till you've been there.

Perhaps the best example of us in human terms is the family. Here, a husband and wife become one and produce a child who possesses commonalities from both parents. They are one family, with three persons.

However, they are not equal in all ways as the Son, Spirit, and I are, nor can they reach the level of intimacy, love, acceptance, and unanimity that the Godhead does.

So how can I explain Myself to you? There is nothing in My Creation that is exactly like Me, nothing that I have created that imitates Me precisely. Only another Godhead would offer an exact view, and such is impossible. I am truly one of a kind. As are you. But just to humor you, imagine three best friends who have always existed. They will never die, they never change in character, they possess equal power and they can do anything they want. They are each a unique mind, soul, and spirit, and yet something about them is intermingled; they possess a unity and oneness that goes beyond friendship, devotion, and respect. They are joined together in the root, something like Siamese Twins, but on a spiritual level. These three friends have probing and towering minds. They converse, they discuss, but not verbally. Each knows the others thoughts and feelings instantly, completely, utterly. We plan all our adventures and creations together, and we debate but always come together in perfect harmony and agreement. Love and holiness mark our relationship in every dimension, and our love is both sacrificial and surpassing, infinite and intimate, spiritual and deeply personal. Only the love of a man for a woman in its highest and most sublime elements comes close to the love that We experience together. Some people have thought that the reason We created the universe and the angelic sphere is because We were lonely and needed to love and be loved. That is not true. The love of God for Son and Son for Spirit is ineffable, inexplicable, inextinguishable, and immeasurable. No creature can fully understand it, and yet it is the thing that makes Creation and mankind possible. Sadly, We could never create a being equal in love to the love We possess, but in redeemed humankind we have come close.

No, I take that back. We haven't come close. But We come away satisfied.

Do You and the Son and the Spirit have sex?

I knew (in more ways than one) you were going to ask that!

To satisfy your curiosity, I will say that Our love, like human sex, includes both ecstasy and intimacy. Sex, as We designed it, was meant to be the ultimate point of pleasure in a love relationship, and it echoed the depths and heights of the love we possess in the Trinity. But do not blaspheme. We do not have intercourse in a physical sense. We are not physical beings, We are spirit, and thus We are so intimately interwoven that ecstasy, joy, jubilation, and pleasure, akin to human orgasm, are Ours in abundance. Everything We do produces joy on a level that in human hearts, as they exist in your sphere, would be uncontainable. They would burst at the merest trickle of spiritual, eternal, divine joy. I have often given those such as you a taste of that joy in the highest, most sublime moments, and inevitably people cry out to be released from it because of its power.

I experienced that once, when I was converted.

It often happens at that time. But there are other moments when I choose to allow a mortal to drink of it.

So I guess You have it pretty good up there.

I can't complain.

Now that sounds like one of the guys down at the bar and grill who just got engaged or something.

Just as you are in My image, so, in many ways, I am in your image. The thing we learned in Jesus was that humans do not like to be talked down to. Plus, I did a little too much complaining and threatening in the early days.

About Israel?

About everyone.

You made a mistake?

Hmmmm.

Come on. Did You make a mistake?

On a human level, I sometimes overreacted. From a divine level, I knew all along exactly what I was doing. It's hard to explain. On a divine level, I see everything from an eternal perspective. I knew the end from the beginning. We plotted out every detail of the plan long before We enacted it. Working on a human level, though, is different. Time is different. One moment follows the other. People act, react, change, divert, evaluate, reevaluate, start, stop, consider, reconsider. It's a mess working with a human being. The hardest part is explaining how divine sovereignty and human freedom work together. They're like train tracks. They are both always there. They both get to the same destination. They never quite intersect. And they are both necessary. Humans are always trying to get the two to work in perfectly logical harmony, but they can't, to a human mind. It's either one or the other. For God, it is both.

Thus, to truncate a long story, from a human perspective it does indeed appear that I have made some mistakes. From a divine perspective, though, everything is working toward the end I've devised, and nothing is amiss.

Methinks thou dost protest too much.

I knew you would say that. In fact, I knew it before you were ever created. And what is My answer? So be it. You'll think what you want to think. Just understand that in every human-God relationship, I must do things that on the surface appear one way but in reality are quite different. Seen from one perspective, it looks like a mistake, or evil, or foolish. Seen from a second perspective, it all makes sense. Like the father in the parable of the prodigal son. Seen from one perspective, the father looks like a dolt, an old fool who has no control over his children; who is manipulated into giving in to a strident, ridiculous, and illegal demand; who spends his days pining for the boy who went wrong. Seen from another perspective, we see a wise father who knew his son could only grow up and be truly redeemed through being let go. What is that bumper sticker I see on cars these days: "If you love something, let it go free. If it doesn't come back, hunt it down and kill it." Pretty sad commentary on humanity, but it does speak of a subtle truth. If you try to force someone you love into a grid, they will often rebel and hate you for it. It's better to let them go. Going back to My original point, the same event appears two different ways to two different observers. On many occasions in ancient times I railed against the people of Israel for their disobedience, their idolatry, their inhumanity. Read through the prophets, and it seems I do little else but threaten and condemn. Why did I deal with them that way? Because other efforts proved futile. I chose to get a message out that evil would not be tolerated. I followed through on My threats, and people were brought to faith. Only a remnant, but a few. Those few

are like precious gems in My treasuries. I would not exchange them for all the gold of Egypt. (Of course, nowa-
days Egypt doesn't have much gold, just old tombs, but
it's an old expression. Fort Knox is another good alterna-
tive, but that also is being depleted. Seems like no one has
gold these days except New York stockbrokers. Maybe I'll
just have to make a change in terminology.)

I think you get My point just the same.

You didn't make any mistakes.

As your president's spin-doctors say, "No comment."

*It would be kind of nice for You to admit You made a mistake or
two, but that's scary. If You made one or two, how many more are
You making right now? And with my life?*

Touché. You see the dilemma. But let Me reiterate: I make
no mistakes with My people. You are in good hands. You
can trust that I know where I'm going and I know how to
get you there.

Maybe we'd better talk about something else.

I detect some doubt.

I'm not satisfied with Your answer.

And how should I answer—say that I've sinned, I've blown
it, I've blown it numerous times, I'm a boob, don't follow
Me? Say that I've made a mess of planet earth, it's a hopeless case, destroy it? Say that the whole Creation was a
misguided adventure, we should start over?

Well, no.

But that is where it would lead.

I suppose.

Then let Me clear the air. I am infallibly wise, infinitely holy, and utterly loving. I plotted every detail of the human saga, and it is all running to a conclusion I planned before I ever began. If for a moment I didn't think I could pull it off, I would no longer be God. To some, the death of Jesus on the cross was a colossal mistake. To others, it is the defining moment of history, the moment that makes history possible. I will continue to try to persuade the former of their error, and I applaud the latter for their insight. I know that at the end, all will see the wisdom of My plan. But I have to be patient. Frequently, your own SuperBowl looks like a done deal after the first touchdown drive. That happened in 1998 with the Packers and the Broncos (I'm a Broncos fan, mind you, despite John Elway), but believe Me I did nothing to help either side win. At the beginning, after that first touchdown, it appeared that what everyone predicted (a Packers rout) was happening. But it didn't happen. Like others of you have said, "It ain't over till the fat lady sings." I'm the fat lady, and I haven't sung yet, but I've played some tunes and they have gone precisely as I planned. One day I will sing, and it will be a song you'll never forget. No honest judge can rule on a case until he's heard all the available facts. One day, I will make all the facts available, and then everyone, and I mean EVERYONE, will have a chance to come to a conclusion. Until then, I advise you, for My sake and your sanity, refuse to judge. Let the fat lady have her song. And when she's done, you can give her a thumb's up or a thumb's down.

So let Me relieve your doubts: I know what I'm doing.

Trust Me. I'll get you there. Remember, "there" is where the real fun begins. At the conclusion, all will make sense, and every thought, word, and deed will be brought to light. Every wrong will be righted, and every trouble will be evaluated, understood, and corrected. Every pain anyone has borne will be salved, and every suffering soul will find hope and charity. I have planned it so, and I will make it happen.

I do trust You.

Good. Why don't you go have a nice dinner and we'll continue after you've gotten a God-ordained steak under your belt?

Good idea. God-ordained steak?

All of them are.

Why You Love Us

Sometimes I wonder, Father, why do You care about us? I mean, we're basically a bunch of ingrates who, if You didn't seek us, would probably be perfectly content to spend our lives in degrading romps through the glades of earth, swilling junk food, getting drunk, and making as much of the sexual revolution as the horrors of AIDs and other things will allow. What makes You love us so? Are we intrinsically lovable?

Not at all. In fact, when I meet most of you, or should I say, when you meet Me, you're usually on the down side of life, in trouble, and looking for someone to fix up your latest disaster. Most of you are, as one of My favorite humorists has said (and despite his lack of respect for Me),

"If you pull a dog out of the gutter, and give him food, a house to roam, and a new family, he will not bite you in return. This is the principle difference between a dog and a man." I've been bitten many times. I find humanity intrinsically unlovable, irascible, always getting into trouble, and intensely self-centered. When you know them as I do—all their worst moments right in front of My eyes from all eternity—you quickly realize this is not a kindly race of people.

Come on, we're not all that bad?

That's just the point. You're not all THAT bad, but you're all bad on one level or another. As one theologian has said, trying very hard to simplify the issue of original sin: you're not all as bad as you could be, but you're as bad off as you could be. It all has to do with the sin pattern and desire that each of you inherited as an heir of your first parents, Adam and Eve.

So they were real?

Of course they were real.

There's a lot of argument about that these days.

Scientists in your age think they have cornered the market on truth. But let's not get into that right now. I don't want you to shut your mind off because I've expressed some views you don't find particularly savory. What I'm saying is that when Adam and Eve sinned in the first garden, the Garden of Eden, they experienced a sudden and humanly irreversible spiritual catastrophe: they became infinitely distant and distrustful of Me; they became prone to sinful attitudes and desires; and they became, at the core of their being, angry, confused, disorganized souls. They no longer knew what the truth was. Have you ever heard the expression that a liar suffers two terrible consequences of his lies: one, no one believes him; two, he can't believe anybody else. Liars think that everyone is a liar because they are one. And liars thrive on untruth. Adam and Eve began lying, accusing, and blaming one another the moment they ate of the tree of the knowledge of good and evil. As a result, they distrusted one another, they distrusted Me, and they became utterly isolated in their world. They could not make each other understand what was inside of them, because they couldn't be honest with each other. As a result, they were the first two desperately lonely people.

You sound like You pity them.

Pity? God doesn't pity people. I know too much about them to pity them. They were reaping what they had sown. It's a law I've placed deep into the fabric of the universe. What you sow is what you reap. If you sow the wind, you will reap the whirlwind.

I'm not sure, but I'm detecting something here, a bitterness perhaps?

No bitterness. Adam and Eve were My greatest achievement. I knew before I created them that they would sin. I knew before I put them in the Garden that they would make all the wrong choices. But that doesn't change the fact that they were perfect, flawless creatures, and the crown of My Creation.

If they were perfect, why did they choose the wrong thing?

For a moral choice to be both a moral and a real choice, I could not force them to go one way or the other. For them it had to be real, something they could not only intellectualize but feel in the depths of their spirit. The choice was whether to obey Me and trust Me, or obey and trust someone else. In this case, Satan. I gave them ample warning. I told them the consequences of a wrong choice. Adam in particular knew all the ramifications of what he was doing. But he rejected Me and wisdom for the woman and Satan's deceit.

But why?

Because he had the right and privilege. It was his to choose. His choice. No one forced him either way. The decision sat squarely on his shoulders. Every moral choice in life is like that. There are always two ways to go: My way and the way of evil. You can call it his way, Adam's way, or "your" way, but in reality it's not yours at all. You are just playing into forces that tempt and deceive you in order to lead you down their path. Ultimately, there are only two ways in this world when it comes to moral choices: My way and Satan's way. Follow Me or Satan. It's your choice. You alone can make it. It's both your right and your privilege, but it is fraught with danger.

What do You mean by "moral choice"?

A choice that involves a good, right way and an evil, wrong way. Tom's father tells Tom to milk the cow. Tom has a moral choice: to obey or play. He decides to play. Later, his father catches him and asks, "What are you doing? Did you milk the cow?" Tom has another moral choice: to lie or to tell the truth. He lies. His father goes to the barn, and finds the milk pail empty. He says, "You will now be punished." He gives the boy a whipping. The boy is confronted with another moral choice: to complain and be angry, or to accept and admit his wrongdoing. Simple action. Three moral choices. Life is full of them. I'd say the average person has at least a hundred moral choices every day. In every case, I will warn him to do right through his heart and his conscience. In many cases, he will reject My counsel and do wrong. Then he'll get caught and be angry that he got caught. He'll make excuses, blame others, and say that everyone was wrong but himself. Moral choices are everywhere. But Adam and Eve had only one. Nothing else in their lives involved a moral choice. Nothing. To eat an orange or an apple? No problem. Choose one or the other. It was a neutral choice. To pet the lion or the zebra. Either way, it's okay. No moral choice.

But there was one real, honest-to-goodness moral choice in all the multitude of decisions they made every day. Just one. Would they follow Me, or another? They had to have that choice, because it was all around them, in everything they did. They were not robots. I could not make them go one way or the other. They were entirely free creatures, and they had a real choice. In the end, they thought they were following their own desires, but they weren't. They simply played into the hands of Satan, who would use them for his own ends against Me.

Why didn't You stop them?

I warned them repeatedly about the consequences of a wrong choice. They knew death would follow rebellion. But if I had stepped in, if I had loosened the fruit from their hands, if I had made them spit out the bite they'd taken, they'd just have had to face the same choice the next minute, or the next hour, or the next day. No, I had to let them make their real choice on their own terms. It is the only way with truly free creatures who are made in My image.

But why? What if You had stopped them? Then the world would not be the way it is.

Yes, it would be populated by robots. People who do My bidding without thinking, without feeling, without the least shred of love or hate, integrity or virility. What kind of world is that?

No, I wanted people who were like Me: free of the coercions of evil, free to love and give and sacrifice, free to choose truth over wrong, free to live joyously in the knowledge that you are the real thing, a person made in the image of God. You see love is not possible without moral choices. Worship is not possible without moral choices. Nothing that matters is possible without moral choices. And if I never gave Adam and Eve or anyone else a real moral choice, they would never really be people with dignity and composure and wisdom and courage and anything else that makes life life. Without a real choice, they would never have achieved their real potential as human beings. In fact, they wouldn't be human; they'd be humanoids. Things. Animals without choices, operating on instinct that I put inside them to help them survive. Little more than fleshly computers.

Okay, so You don't love us because we're lovable. Do You love us because of the potential You see in us?

There is no potential apart from Me. When you become

one with Me, you have potential. Otherwise, all is dust and death.

Then why do You love us?

Because.

That's a father's answer to a four-year-old, not an answer. Why?

Because I chose to.

But why did You choose to?

Because of who I am. Because of what I am.

You're love itself.

Yes.

But do You love us because we are Your creations?

Of course.

All right. But there must be some simpler reason.

Child, before you ever were, I knew you. Before you had ever done anything right or wrong, I wanted you for My own. Before you had any potential, before anyone else saw in you a glimmer of greatness or even goodness, I saw you as a helpless child, and I loved you. You had nothing to commend yourself to Me. You had no kingly realm or position. You had no fame or fortune or honor that would impress. I loved you because I LOVE YOU. It is that simple. I am love, and I cannot cease to love anyone anywhere. It is because of who I am, not because of who you are.

So You have always loved me, us, all of us?

That can never change.

Then I guess we really don't have anything to worry about.

That's what I've been trying to tell you!

Dilemmas
Of The Human Mind

EVIL, SUFFERING, AND SO ON

Evil

I want to know about evil, Lord.

Of course. So do they all.

I'm not being facetious.

Neither am I.

Okay, the way I figure it is, however the universe happened, ultimately You created everything.

Correct.

And there was no evil at the beginning.

Correct.

But then evil happened without You causing it.

Right.

All right, how did evil happen? If it just invaded of its own will and screwed things up on its own, it must either be more powerful than You, or else You chose not to stop it, in which case You must not be very loving, seeing all the carnage evil has caused.

The classic question.

What's that?

The classic question of evil. Since evil exists, it means either that God is loving but not all-powerful and therefore can't do anything about it, or else God is all-powerful but not loving, because obviously He hasn't done anything about it. If He were both loving and all-powerful, evil wouldn't and couldn't exist.

Yes, that's what I mean.

First of all, let's get some things straight. If I'm not all-powerful, you and I have a big problem.

What's that?

If I'm not all-powerful, I'm little more than a bigger version of you, and you already know how weak you are. Thus, if all I have is a little more power than you, why should you obey or worship Me? I'm certainly not awe-inspiring in such a scenario, and in all probability, if you got enough of yourselves together, you could overthrow Me and go on and have a wonderful time without any of My restrictions. The result is that if I'm not all-powerful, I'm not much of a god to begin with. Chances are also that I could do little to help you. I could do nothing to change your life situation. So why would you come to Me in the first place?

Yeah, I can see that.

Now, taking the other track, if I'm not loving in the classic sense—unconditionally seeking the highest benefit of all My children—then why are you even spending time talking to Me? If I'm not loving, we couldn't talk, because I wouldn't want to waste My time on you. I'd be off working on My own projects, merrily satisfying Myself to utter oblivion. If I'm not loving, I am little more than a tyrant, or worse, a Nazi Dr. Mengele performing experiments on My mice.

So what are You saying?

I'm saying the very fact that you come to Me and talk like this shows you think that I care and that I can do something about your needs. That means ultimately I must love you and have the resources to change your world. It's not that much of a leap to saying I'm perfectly loving and also all-powerful.

Then the classic question is . . .

Wrong.

What do You mean?

I mean the question assumes that evil could not exist in a universe operated by a perfectly loving and all-powerful God. So He must be only one or the other, or neither. In which case, He's ultimately irrelevant. But the truth is that I am both perfectly loving and all-powerful, and I have allowed evil to exist for other reasons.

What other reasons?

It's complicated.

Try me.

All right, one reason is that I couldn't stop it.

What? I thought You were all-powerful.

Just because I'm all-powerful does not mean I can do anything. For instance, do you know the boulder story?

No.

It's another supposedly classic argument. It states that if God is all-powerful, could He create a rock so big that He Himself could not lift it?

So?

Well, the question doesn't make sense because it assumes I'm nothing but all-powerful. The fact is that I am many things, among them wise. And I would immediately ask the question, what good would creating such a rock do? First of all, it would clutter things up.

Heaven knows we have enough of that!

Right. Second, whom would it benefit?

The scholars who made up the question?

Indeed. So My wisdom and My omnipotence must work together, and one militates against the other, counseling Me not to make such a rock. So such a rock couldn't be created because it's foolish. And there's still another problem.

What's that?

> If such a rock could be created it would have to be infinite, for I am infinite, and it's impossible for two infinite things to occupy the same space. So that's a second count against it. But there's a third problem.

Yes?

> If such a rock could be created, it would also have to contain all the attributes of God to be greater than God. It wouldn't just be a rock anymore, but it would be holy, immutable, omnipresent, omniscient, all those things. And that would mean I wasn't God. The rock would be God.

I'm getting confused.

> Good. That means you're thinking.

So where does that leave the evil issue?

> Right where we started. I am both loving and all-powerful, and therefore evil exists for other reasons.

Of which You gave me one.

> Yes.

That You couldn't prevent evil from invading the universe.

> Correct.

But why couldn't You?

> Let Me tell you a story.
> It was to be the greatest orchestra in Creation. Magnificent beyond words. Beyond even the music itself. The best musicians. The most fantastic pieces to play and per-

form. A flawless, creative, and masterful conductor.

And of course, the most appreciative audience ever: the owner, his son, and the great uncle. They had conceived it. Now they would create it, instrument by instrument, musician by musician, piece by piece, performance by performance. They would do it.

And why? Nothing less than glory. Sublime, perfect, ineffable glory. Forever and ever.

The owner set about his work. He, the son, and the great uncle distributed the duties, but essentially all three would work together, sometimes helping, sometimes leading. The grand idea fixed itself in all three of their minds as though one.

They built the stage, a marvelous stratification of hues and jewels—chrysolite, ebony, sapphire, ruby, diamond— light would go through it and illumine each note, set the music in its most sublime profundity effortlessly.

The three seats stood out before the stage like three thrones. But the owner did not think of them as thrones so much as a place to reap the rich reward of Creation's greatest melodies and harmonies.

The son took charge of the instruments, each a marvelous blending of wood, metal, jewel, fabric, string, leather, and wind. There would be myriads of them, myriads of each type, and myriads of the myriads. Each became the perfect product of a skilled craftsman, the son himself.

The great uncle initiated the composition of the music. The pieces would combine every musical note, tone, chord, arrangement, riff, pitch, and modulation imaginable— compositions so varied, so flawless, so beautiful, so new and rising and inexplicable that the musicians themselves would burn to perform every waking moment.

The owner took special care of the development of the musicians, their nurture, study, and expansion, until they performed effortlessly and with a perfection beyond words. The music could be nothing less than the product of myriads of hearts, souls, minds, and strengths united into one vast symphonic crescendo of joy and beauty.

The conductor himself received the benefits of the mental and spiritual acumen of all three of his leaders. For years on end they labored to hone and polish him till he shone upon his podium like the sun. Even as he moved, light refracted from his garments like the very music itself. Perfect. Beautiful. An eye and ear sensation.

It was not long before all was ready.

The conductor stood at the podium. He raised his baton. Every musician stood ready to burst forth with that first vibrant andante.

It was not at all disappointing. They played on and on, the compositions reaching higher, plunging deeper, unifying the most tantalizing of melodies and harmonies. Even the owner sat back astonished and grateful. A tear fell from his eye as he listened. It was his greatest achievement, his moment.

For days on end they played, the orchestrations punctuated by sharp romps of individual and small group performance. Different musicians worked together with the conductor. For them the owner created special compositions, spurts of gratitude and joy that thrilled the son and the great uncle as much as the owner himself.

The joy of performance was so great that none in the whole orchestra tired for a moment of going on. Even when a duet, trio, quartet, or soloist made a special performance, it was the gathered company—all playing and rising to the highest of crescendos—as they entered into the arrangement with the greatest abandon, that they began to worship and enjoy the fellowship like wind through fir, or pure water gently rolling down a mountainside.

The owner, his son, and the great uncle could not have been more pleased.

But very few things in Creation go perfectly forever, and even this august gathering suffered a fracture. Almost imperceptible at first, it was something unnameable, inexplicable.

Of course, the owner knew. From the start. So did the son and the great uncle. But it dragged away at their hearts and many times they wished it could be otherwise.

It was the conductor. No one in the orchestra questioned his position of authority, or his intellect, or his choices for the time and place of each performance. No one questioned his integrity. Or his perfection. Or his right to silence one and give another the first place.

Their eyes fixed on him in a calm willingness to follow.

But they all knew for whom they performed. They knew that ultimately even the conductor was an employee.

And that was where the irk arose. "Employee." Some even dared to whisper the word, "servant." Never to his face. For they all knew if he was "servant," they were something even less.

Of course, the owner never spoke in such terms. His words had a more majestic ring. "Covering cherub." "Anointed seraph." "Angel." "Principality." "Power."

But somehow the word "servant" cut its way into the conductor's conversation like an sharp-edged knife. He never said anything to the owner, just dropped a hint here, a thought there.

"Does it ever cross your mind that . . ."

"Do you ever think about the fact that . . ."

"Have you ever considered the possibility of . . ."

The conductor was such a handsome, dignified presence that no one dared question what was happening. It was thought to be a mere mistake, some faulty tuning of a violin that simply needed to be gently corrected.

This the owner sought to do. He spent long sessions coaching and quietly talking with the conductor. It served as both a fatherly bit of advice, and a warning. "This course you are setting yourself on," the owner said, "do you understand that it ends in death?"

The conductor only turned away, sullen. He spoke of "freedom," and "doing what he wanted to do," and "finding his own way."

The owner only said that he would find such things in time, as he learned to completely express his gifts. "Freedom," he said, "is doing what is right and best, not what you wish."

The conductor only scowled.

Soon it began infiltrating the music. He purposely switched harmonies on some pieces, changed a melody here and there, made demands on the musicians that even the owner didn't raise. Of course, his changes grated on the beauty of the music. It was nearly ruined by the strokes he put in.

Naturally, it was nearly imperceptible at first—to most of the other musicians. And it was done all in the name of a better performance.

But the performances were not better. They were marred by a critical spirit, an antagonistic attitude that could not be mistaken.

Soon it was plain. The conductor hated the owner.

Repeatedly, the owner warned him. "Please think long and hard about what you're doing and saying. It's not helping you or anyone else." And, "you do understand that if this continues I will have to take action."

The conductor only sneered behind his back.

The owner decided to relax his rein a little more and to give the conductor more room to "find his way," as he called it.

But the conductor kept pushing the rein back.

Soon, it was clear: he didn't want just freedom to perform or to do as he pleased. He wanted nothing to do with the owner. In fact, he wanted to take the owner's place completely.

It was a startling revelation.

The owner, his son, and the great uncle talked long hours into the day and night. They knew what the end was. But the conductor seemed bent on his course. And, short of destruction or elimination, he wouldn't listen to any plea.

But then he suddenly switched tacks. He became the model conductor, doling out the music perfectly, though mechanically. Many thought that a real change had occurred. The conductor had found the right way. His previous fits were just missed notes in an otherwise perfect rendition of the owner's work.

But the joy was gone. If the perfection remained, nonetheless, the heart had been cut out of it. Performing had become a chore, for everyone concerned.

Yes, some played with all their heart. But to see so many so black and angry, blowing and bowing and plucking their perfect notes with such virulence tore the very soul out of everything.

The conductor had a perfect explanation for the musicians who approached him about the problem. "The owner requires of me preposterous things."

He gave his spiel over and over. "The owner doesn't know what he's talking about." "The owner is no musician," unlike the conductor, of course. "The owner has taken too hard a hand. No freedom for anyone."

Soon, questions were flying. The conductor had ready answers. "We can form our own orchestra. We can play what we want." To each, he privately promised special rewards. "First violinist." "First trombone." "First cellist." "The seat closest to the front." "A chance to compose and perform your own music."

Soon, the whole orchestra was abuzz with talk about some "major changes."

Some considered it dead wrong and hoped the owner would do something soon. But others weren't sure. What the conductor said seemed plausible, and attractive.

It was then that several of the loyal musicians went to the owner. Did he know what was happening? Had he seen the change? Was he aware of the criticism going on behind his back?

He knew.

They were astonished.

"What are you going to do about it?"

He said he was working on it. Not to worry.

But it all dragged at the owner's heart, and he had many more conferences with the son and the great uncle. Finally, a meeting was called. The owner gave a speech. Musicianship. Getting back to basics. Commitment. The joy of excellence. Performance.

They listened raptly. It seemed to be back to the old order.

Many were content.

But the conductor went back to working between the performances. He spoke to each of them in corners, back rooms, behind the stage. It was soon clear who had taken his side and who had taken the owner's.

"What do we do?" one of them asked at a special secret meeting of the "new order," as they called themselves.

"I say we take him," said the conductor. "Straight out."

Some gasped and left. Others were all for it. Nearly a third of the orchestra had joined him.

"Look at him," said the conductor. "Compare him and me. Or the son. Or that old uncle. Don't you think we can take them? It'll be over in a minute. One solid crack to the jaw and he's done."

It was true. Neither the owner, the son, or the great uncle looked anything like the conductor, or even most of the musicians. True, when they walked into the assembly, the whole place lit up. But it was the orchestra that danced the dance of light. Not them. They, in fact, were hardly noticeable. Even rumpled looking.

The conductor decided to bring it off. He and his loyalists laid out elaborate plans. Secret missions went on. Those loyal to the conductor spent long sessions arguing with opposing musicians, trying to win them over.

Strangely, the owner said nothing. He seemed merely to be waiting for what might happen. So also the son, and the great uncle.

It was all planned for an evening's performance. On a certain note, every loyalist would jump up with his weapon—an instrument, a sharpened jewel, a chair—and dispatch the specific two or three he most hated. Everyone had an assignment.

That evening, the performance was going better than usual. The notes and melodies rang out with a precision not witnessed in some time.

But suddenly at the height of a certain allegro, the conductor turned on his podium, made a sweep with his baton, and jumped at the audience, the baton suddenly transformed into a hideous sword of light. He went straight for the owner's throat.

Instantly, the whole stage was thrown into a boiling cauldron of anger. Musicians hurled instruments and chairs, gnashed their teeth, flailed away with arms, legs, and hands. Some had sharpened knives and other weapons.

Soon, broken bodies lay everywhere. Private scores were settled. Battles raged all over the platform.

Even the owner seemed to have some trouble fending off the enraged conductor with several of the conductor's specially selected henchman.

But in the end, a dividing line came up between them and two groups stood on either side, taunting, yelling, and panting.

Most of the instruments were broken, unusable. The stage was a mess. Amazingly, no one died. The owner himself, the son, and the great uncle escaped harm. No one quite knew how.

As the two forces stood panting and shrieking, the owner called for silence. He stood in their midst, facing the conductor and the opposing forces behind him.

"So you have chosen to rebel and fight?"

The conductor nodded, saliva and blood dripping from his chin. "We just want our own place, our own orchestra. To do as we please. We don't want to perform for you any longer."

"Why should I grant this?" said the owner, coolly calm.

The conductor laughed. "You don't grant it. We take it."

The owner chewed his lip. "And if I let you live, what will you do?"

"First, we'll get rid of you permanently!" shouted someone behind the conductor. But the conductor waved for silence.

"We'll play our own music."

"You won't bother the group that remains loyal to me?"

"No," said the conductor. "We'll mind our own business."

"So be it," said the owner. "We shall see what you do. But you are not to play here."

A gasp went up from those behind him. But a cheer rose from the group with the conductor.

A place was agreed upon for the conductor and his group to perform to their own satisfaction.

The two groups parted.

In the course of time, the owner gave all the loyalists new instruments and new music. They were playing beautifully.

But the conductor and his henchmen had a problem. No one could compose. And no one had an instrument. They couldn't play a note. Furthermore, they had no stage. And without the creative powers of the owner, they seemed at a loss of what to do.

However, the conductor had a plan. He organized them into gangs and began attacking lone musicians, invading quarters, making thefts. Many of the loyal musicians were harmed, lost their instruments, and had their fingers or their lips smashed. Although the owner was able to balm and heal their wounds, it was apparent that he had to do something. His own musicians were being hurt, losing their instruments, and in some cases, they were being turned against him.

Then they learned that the conductor intended to take the stage, all the instruments they could take, and do their best to destroy the owner and all that now belonged to him.

A decision had to be made, final action taken.

The owner gathered the loyalists, the son, and the great uncle together.

"We have a reached a point of no return. We cannot let things go on as they are. The conductor and his people are attacking and hurting ours mercilessly. We have to decide what to do."

"Can you just get rid of them altogether?" asked one of the musicians who had been brutally battered the night before, losing a precious violin in the process.

"Yes," said the owner. "I can eliminate them entirely."

The whole group gasped as one. "You can?!" shouted one.

"Then why haven't you?" asked another.

"I want to discuss the options," said the owner. "So you understand. One is that I eliminate them entirely."

"Bravo!" rang from the galleries.

The owner paced before them. "But it's not an option without its difficulties," he said. "For instance, who's to say I won't appoint another conductor who will do the same as this first one has done. We could go on and on like that for years until your numbers are so depleted, we wouldn't even have an orchestra."

Everyone was silent.

Then someone else said, "Banish them! Send them somewhere else. Give them their own place."

The owner nodded. "That's a legitimate thought. But

that is what we have already done, and it hasn't worked. They do not have the power to create, as I do, and so they must get their own music, instruments, and place to perform by theft, trickery, and murder."

That was all true.

But the owner went on. "Anyway, don't I have a responsibility to those over there? Even though they've rejected me, I hear they're already fighting among themselves. Soon there will be splinter groups there too. In no time they'll all be asking for their own place, their own orchestras. It would go on and on like this forever."

The group appeared rather dejected. Then someone said, "Why not give them another chance to come back?"

This time the son spoke up. "We've already given them that chance. They don't want it."

"Maybe in time they will," said the same musician.

"Perhaps. But how long are we to wait?" asked the great uncle. "How many of our people will be hurt and maimed?"

There seemed no way.

But then the owner looked out over the group. "I will now tell you what I have decided to do. But it is a plan not without its hazards—for all of us. My goal is that in the end you will all see that I am indeed worthy of the loyalty you have already shown me. I am grateful for that. And I promise I won't misuse it."

He paused, and someone said, "What are you going to do, sir?"

"We will let them make their own way—for the time being," said the owner.

"But that means they'll be attacking us in their hit squads!" shouted another.

The owner shook his head. "No, I'll see to it that that

stops. No, we will let them make their own music."

The whole gathering gasped.

"Yes, they will have a complete crack at it. Any way they want to play, they can play. I will make them their own stage and their own place to perform. They will have a complete chance to play every variation of their kind of music that they desire. Of course, they will have to come up with it all on their own. Just the same, they'll have a chance to show just how well their system works. I'll give them every opportunity to prove that their music is better and their orchestration is superior."

He stopped and looked out over the bedraggled audience.

Then he went on. "In the process, you—all of you—will take notes, make comparisons between them and us. And in the end, I'll let you make your own judgment—whether you want to stick with me, or go over to their side."

The group was silent. Then someone asked, "But will this just go on like this forever?"

The owner smiled. "No. There will be an end. I'll give everyone ample warning. But someday they, and you, will be called to account for what you have done with what I gave you."

"A judgment you mean."

"Yes."

There was a vast silence.

"Then, what happens now?"

"I'll explain it all to them, and then we begin. The grand experiment, we'll call it. The final proof. My way. . . ."

There was another long pause.

"Or their way. You will all choose." The owner quietly looked into every pair of eyes.

"On with it, then," someone said suddenly.

The owner grimaced. "It will not be easy work. They will still try to attack and hurt us."

"But why, sire? Why do they hate us so?"

The owner looked at them a long time. Finally, he shook his head. "Even I do not understand it. But it is part of what it means to be a musician, free under my care and in my kingdom. Everyone has a choice."

There was a long silence.

Then the owner said, "There is much to do, much to learn, much to prove. Go to it. And we'll report in every day about what we're seeing. Agreed?"

The shout went up uniformly. "Agreed!" And so the grand experiment began.

Bravo! A good story..

It's more than a good story. It's a true story.

The rebellion of Satan?

Yes.

So we are still in the midst of the grand experiment?

Yes.

But I still don't understand why people rebel like that when they had everything.

When I created the beings who populate My universe, I gave them the freedom to choose whether or not to obey Me. I created them as moral beings. That is, they had the power and the responsibility to choose good or bad, right or wrong. Every person, including you, has the power to listen to Me or not, to obey Me or not. I made you that way.

But why? Why didn't You make it so we couldn't choose wrong?

Because then you would have been less than a true moral Being created to know Me and learn of Me. You would be little more than a robot. (Haven't we already had this conversation? But it bears repeating). Sure, I could make it do whatever I wanted. You can take a computer and make it say "I love you," but you know that's not real love, not even close. Anyway, that's not the kind of creature I wanted to create. Computers are easy. Humans are another matter altogether. When I set about creating the world, I wanted creatures who think, who love, who give, who sacrifice when necessary, who value truth and want to do right, who desire to learn and grow and nurture and share. To get such Beings I had to take some risks. I had to risk allowing them true freedom. That meant they could hate Me and rebel against Me as well as love Me and obey Me.

But couldn't You have made us so that we couldn't choose evil?

No. It just doesn't work that way. To get moral Beings on the level I wanted, you have to give them freedom to choose good and evil.

So evil came in because we ultimately chose it.

Yes.

The whole Adam and Eve thing?

In a sense.

In a sense?

It opens up quite a can of worms for people who are living

in your culture, so I don't push it. At the start, anyway.

But Adam and Eve were real?

Yes, they were two people who existed and experienced the first test. They failed and plunged the whole world into a condition of unspirituality and sin that has ultimately led to the condition we find ourselves in today.

Well, I won't push this point.

Thanks.

Thanks?

Yes, I know sooner or later we're going to have to tackle it. And I'm afraid it will lead to a terrific disillusionment on your part.

Then maybe we'd better tackle it now.

No, I'll let it ride. Even the world wasn't made in one day.

All right. I'll leave that to Your discretion.

Gratzi.

Getting back to the question of evil, I'm still a little confused.

So are most of you.

Some say that evil and good are in a constant struggle and one never ultimately wins over the other.

They're wrong.

They are?

Absolutely.

So good ultimately wins?

At the end of everything, yes, good wins.

That's great. I was worried about it.

I know. Don't be. It's all well in hand.

So You have it all worked out?

Yes.

That's good enough for me.

(He laughs.)

Okay, but others have the idea of the Force, like in Star Wars, *as we discussed earlier. We can plug into the evil side or the good side. The Force is neutral. It doesn't pick sides.*

I pick sides.

You do?

Of course. The whole world is plunged into a battle between good and evil. Evil is trying very hard to destroy everything good has done. Evil cannot create, it can only use what good has created. Thus, evil is at somewhat of a disadvantage. It's weaker than good, but it puts up a stout fight.

But when I say good and evil, I'm not talking about two forces. Good is a person: Me. Evil is wrapped up in a person, too: Satan. Satan and I are in a dispute at the moment, and both of us are vying for the souls and hearts of men and women and children.

How are You vying?

I'm trying to convince people that I'm good, I'm worth trusting, and I love them. I showed them the extent of My love in Jesus. He went to the cross to die on their behalf. He died in their place. He laid down his life for each and every person on earth. That's how great his and My love are. We sacrificed our lives. We say, "follow us, and we will give you eternal life, forgiveness, hope, life, friendship, leadership, power, etc." Anyone who follows us gets those things on some level in this life, and in a much higher version in the next.

Kind of like software—the regular version and the deluxe.

You've got it.

So I guess the guy on the other side is Satan.

Correct.

He's busy telling people that I'm no good, I'm not worth trusting, I don't love anyone but myself, and that basically I'm a complete goof not worthy of worship or anything else. He says, "Follow me, and I'll give you whatever you want." So they think if they follow him by doing evil, they'll get what they want. They never do, but it sounds good up front. Once they're locked into evil ways and attitudes, they're very hard to let go. Like a virus.

Interesting. So You and Satan are in this battle?

Yes. Each of us woos the souls and hearts of people. When someone joins My team by believing in My Son, all of heaven rejoices, his name is written in the Book of Life, he becomes a full-fledged citizen of heaven with all its joys and privileges, and he gets My Spirit to be in him and with him every step of the rest of his life on earth.

On the other hand, Satan introduces his followers to all the pleasures of evil. Adultery, illicit wealth, hatred, prejudice, you name it, they experience it.

Who wins?

I do.

Does Satan know this?

Yes. That's why he's fighting so hard at the moment to keep most people from learning about Me and coming to Me for the gift of real life.

If Satan knows this, why does he fight on?

What else can he do? Plus, he believes that somehow he'll still win, even though he knows deep down this is a lie.

Then why doesn't he surrender? Why doesn't he give up, or at least negotiate for a stalemate?

First, because he wants to win. Second, because he knows I won't negotiate anything but a complete and final surrender. Third, because a liar tends to believe his own lies.

But why hasn't it happened yet? It seems like this victory is taking a long time.

When you're working with free creatures, winning the war does take a long time. In addition, I don't want to lose any of My own, so I'm giving everyone plenty of time to decide between Me and Satan.

Satan seems so unreal, though. How do I know I'm not just following my own impulses, my own plan?

Many people are. It seems that way because Satan is invisible, a spirit like Me. He is also subtle. He only reveals himself to those most committed to his side. He's content to let anyone do anything, so long as it isn't what I want them to do. Satan's way is anarchy, democracy, monarchy, tyranny, whatever gets you through the night. He doesn't care so long as it's not theocracy—Me on the throne of the soul. You see in this battle, there are only two sides. He who is not with Me, is with him. And he who is not with him, is with Me.

Take Saddam Hussein.

You can have him.

I don't want him. But think about him. Who's behind his program and plan? Is it Satan?

Ultimately.

Do You love Saddam?

As I love all My creatures. I would like him to come to My Son, to find faith and become a disciple.

Is it possible he will?

Nothing is impossible with God. You may be surprised. But in a case like his, it's very hard. Chuck Colson was a tough nut, though, and I cracked him. So were you.

Me?

When did you become a disciple of Jesus?

At age twenty-one.

See, it took Me twenty-one years to get you.

It seems like it took such a long time. And if You had gotten me earlier, a lot of pain would have been avoided.

It was because of and through the pain that you came to Me. Without the pain you would not have been interested.

Are You saying You couldn't get me before twenty-one?

For every person, when they become a follower of Jesus is the right time, the only time. There is a very small window of opportunity. That is why I always urge people to believe NOW. NOW is the time of salvation. NOW is the hour of belief. You simply do not know what tomorrow will bring or what changes will come into your outlook.

So You're saying if I hadn't become a believer at twenty-one when I did, I would never have become one?

That night in the small room in your parents's basement was the moment of faith for you. No other moment would have been right. You were ready. Your mind and heart were open. I had opened them and prepared you for that minute when your friend asked you if you believed. If you had sluffed off his question, or said, "No, I don't believe that stuff," you may never have had the same opportunity again. For every person there is a moment of decision. When it comes, it is the right moment, the only moment, and if forsaken, there is no guarantee it will happen again.

We are all in great peril, then.

Everyone who lives without faith in Christ is in great peril. It is the essence of life that the most important decision of all is the one that often seems the most trivial, the simplest. But when a heart is awakened to the truth, there can be no other answer. He will say yes unequivocally.

So it's certain that a person You've chosen will believe?

I will not lose one of My own to My enemies.

What about the others?

They have rejected Me at their own peril.

So Satan is serious, and so are You?

Absolutely serious. The most serious anyone can be. There isn't a more important decision in life. None come close. You can marry or not marry and still have a happy life. You can succeed in business, or fail miserably and still be a decent person. You can raise godly children, or ungodly, and still be considered a good citizen. But you cannot spurn the creator of the universe and survive.

Why do these discussions always leave me half-scared out of my wits?

It is a terrifying thing to fall into the hands of the living God.

Is there anything else I should know about the issue of evil that would help?

In the end, evil will be thrust out of Creation and left in only one place where it will be confined and completely impotent to influence others.

Hell.

Correct.

Then, in the end, evil loses.

It has already lost. We're just doing cleanup.

When did it lose?

At the cross.

How so?

The cross dealt with evil finally. All sin was paid for, the decision to accept or reject was made clear, and Satan and his cohorts were stripped of their power to destroy and deceive. All the rest is denouement. We solved the problem of evil once and for all. Those who will join us will reign forever in a world where no evil can tread. Those who hate us will have no power to insult, hate or destroy anyone except themselves.

Sounds like a touchdown to me.

The real Super Bowl happened in 32 A.D.

I'm glad.

So am I.

People Who Ask Me For Things

Is it possible, Father, for a person to come to You, to pray, to believe in You somewhat, but not really to understand any of the truth You've given us?

Quite possible.

Can You illustrate it?

Ah, another story?

Yes. I like Your stories.

All right. Try this one.

Ralph Pyle was a busy guy. He didn't want much. He didn't expect a lot. Not the moon, or the stars, or a home in Malibu. But he did want a little bit of everything. Just a taste. Just enough to know he'd been there.

When he was fourteen years old he went to God and asked Him to hear his prayer. God consented. Ralph said, "Lord, I know that I don't deserve much. And I don't expect a lot. But I would like some things. Just a little bit. This is my request: I'd like my own bedroom away from my brother, some nice furniture, a stocked refrigerator, a boom box, a girlfriend with looks, and a pet or two. Please understand, I'm not asking for everything. Just a *little bit* of everything."

God understood a person wanting something in this world, having a little piece of ground of your own, and so on. He'd even been the one to promise Abraham, Isaac, and Jacob a place. He didn't begrudge a man the basic needs. So He answered Ralph's prayer. He led his parents to give him his own room, a little fridge all his own, a dog, and one of the cheerleaders on the cheerleading squad fell in love with him. Also, two pairs of designer jeans, a pop toaster, a color TV, a stereo and record collection (not the top of the line, mind you, but square middle of the store), and a boom box for the beach. It wasn't the American Dream, but it was comfortable. Ralph was pleased.

Nonetheless, after a few years of living in the lap of mediocrity, Ralph Pyle suddenly decided he wasn't fully satisfied. "What I need is the right to call some shots," he said. "Not all the shots, just some of them. I don't like people bossing me around all the time."

He journeyed again to the throne of God and set

forth his plea. God listened and asked, "What kind of shots do you want to call? Basketball shots? Financial shots? Political shots? People to command and lead? A voice in your church?"

"That's it," said Ralph. "A little bit of all of the above."

God answered quickly. Within a month, Ralph was signed up to vote on a special board at his church. He was also asked to represent the student body at the local PTA meetings. He was nominated for a position in his homeroom class. He became an assistant coach on the basketball team. And he got a job as a trainee at a local hamburger chain restaurant.

Ralph was very happy. But as always, the day came when Ralph sensed something else was missing. He began to realize a little bit of wealth and a chance to call some shots weren't all they were cracked up to be. He contemplated his problem and suddenly he realized, "I don't have any notoriety or fame. No one knows who I am, except, of course, my parents, and a few of the locals. I think if I had a little taste of fame, just a little piece of it, I would be completed."

Again, he set out for God's throne to lay his request at His feet. At first God didn't understand. "I know who you are," He said.

"But this is different," Ralph said. "I'd like to see my name in print. It would be nice if some people around town recognized Me. I'd like them to say, 'There goes Ralph Pyle.'"

The next few years Ralph had the time of his life. One day he was walking along the street with his dog and a Channel 11 News Truck stopped and a reporter interviewed him about a community problem. He didn't know a lot about it, but he knew a little bit, and he told them what he knew. He was on TV that night. The reporter even said, "You've given me some good quotes."

Later, his picture was in the paper when he received an award for his work as a trainer for the football team. His fiancée cut it out and put it in her scrapbook. People began to take note of Ralph Pyle. Not many people. But a few. Just enough to give Ralph a taste.

Still, Ralph was getting into his early twenties now and he realized something remained wrong. "I have a little bit of wealth, power, and fame. But something's missing."

This time he thought for nearly three months. He even went to the pastor for some counseling.

Through him and other insights, he came to the conclusion that what he lacked was love. He'd never really experienced love—not like in the movies. Oh, he thought highly of his fiancée. She was pretty and loving and she knew how to kiss. But she nagged him now and then. He liked his family a lot. But they were often a bother, especially when he wanted to listen to music in his room. He wanted to feel real love for everyone.

He went to God again and laid it all out before Him.

"You mean you want to be able to love like the nuns in Calcutta who take care of lepers?" God asked excitedly.

Ralph crinkled up his eyes. "I wasn't thinking of that."

"Then you must mean you want to learn to be patient, kind, not jealous, and so on?" God asked again.

Ralph cocked his head. "In a way," he said. "But I wouldn't want it to become a bother."

God appeared dismayed, but asked a last question. "I guess you don't mean the kind of love that leads a person to give up his whole bank account to help someone in need?"

"Oh, no," said Ralph. "Not that. It's . . . it's the kind of love . . ."

". . . that has a warm feeling in your heart for everyone," said God, completing the sentence.

"That's it," said Ralph, looking up. "How did you know?"

God sighed deeply. "You ask a hard thing, Ralph Pyle. But yes, I know the kind of love you want. I've seen much of it. I guess I've always found a way to supply them. So why not you?" He said, shaking his head. "Go your way. I'll try to answer."

The answer was slow in coming. But gradually, Ralph noticed that he began to have nice feelings towards some people. He found he actually liked a lot of people. Not to the point that he really did anything for them. But he began to describe himself as a humanitarian. "I care about the race," he said. "I hope we all get it together."

But, of course, it wasn't enough. He still lacked something. After nearly a year of thinking about it, one morning it hit him. He was nearly thirty. "I don't have faith," he exclaimed to his wife. "I must go to God and talk with Him immediately about it."

"I lack faith," he told the Almighty. "I want some faith."

"Do you want the faith that moves mountains?" asked God, pleased.

"Oh, not all that much," said Ralph, smiling. "I just want enough faith to get me to heaven."

God's face took on a dark look. "Do you not want the faith that takes up its cross and follows My Son wherever He goes?"

"Not that much," replied Ralph. "Just enough to keep me out of hell."

God appeared angry, but Ralph kept smiling. He'd done

everything else, he thought.

"Do you want the faith that obeys My word, studies My truth, and yearns for righteousness, meekness, abundant life?"

Ralph said, "The abundant life part, yes. But those other things I don't think I really need. I just want enough faith to make me a decent American."

God sighed a long, heavy, dark sigh. He said, "Ralph Pyle, you ask the impossible. There is no such faith."

Ralph laughed. "That cannot be, your Majesty. I've seen this faith everywhere I go."

God shook his head. "Yes, you have seen it. But you have not seen faith. What you ask is impossible. I can give you no such faith. Go your way."

At first, Ralph was greatly dismayed. But then he said to himself, "God can't be right. All these people can't be wrong. Maybe He just had a bad day."

So Ralph lived his faith. And it was a rather fun faith. He was always asking God for things after that: to relieve a headache; to get a raise at work; a parking space on a crowded Saturday. Sometimes God answered, sometimes He didn't. But when he did, Ralph always was most pleased and even told the church about it. He became one of the church's best members.

But it wasn't enough faith to get him to heaven. It wasn't enough to keep him out of hell. It was just enough to make him think he had it made. And that he had a little bit of everything.

You tell some rip-snortin' stories Father.

My specialty.

I've seen that kind of faith here and there, too.

It's all over the place. But it's not real faith.

It must make You sad.

Very.

I wish I could do something about it.

Simply believe, My son. Believe and live out the truth of that belief.

I will.

Then you will have pleased Me.

Those Who Have Never Heard

One of the toughest questions people ask about Your Son is how You can condemn people to hell who have never heard of Him. I mean, He lived almost 2,000 years ago. Yet, in that time, millions of people have perished who never heard one word about Him. Furthermore, in the world today there are only about a billion and a half believers in Christ. That leaves three and a half billion who are something else. Many of them have never heard an iota about Jesus, or worse, they've heard all sorts of wrong things about Him. Are these people all destined for hell?

Let's deal with people who have never heard. Either they lived in a place and time where no one could bring them the message, or else they never crossed paths with someone who could give them the message. However it happened, they never heard. What am I to do with them?

There are a number of ways to express faith in this world.

For instance, many Old Testament saints never understood the truth about the Messiah even though I had given them the Bible. But having an actual scroll of the Bible was rare. Few people really understood the nature of Jesus until He actually came, and even then plenty of controversy surrounded His identity. Today, twenty centuries later, people continue to argue about who and what He was, what He came to do, and whether He will come again.

In addition, many people know very few facts about Him, even those who supposedly grew up in a Biblically-based culture like yours. Multitudes of people have heard a few things about Jesus, many of them wrong, and thus cannot make an informed decision about believing in Him.

So what are we to do? The point I was trying to make earlier is that faith has always existed on a number of levels. Adam and Eve had faith in a single promise I made to them: that the "seed of the woman" would crush the "serpent's head." They understood nothing of a virgin birth, of a Son who would die, of a Savior. They only knew someone would come along sometime and redeem humanity. The faith in that promise was all I asked for at that time. Anyone who took Me at My word was redeemed and made a citizen of My kingdom.

I have also spoken to people through conscience, through My law written on their hearts, through their own prophets and priests who served the one true God, even though they knew little about Me. Those people who exercised faith in Me through the understanding they gained through their conscience and Me speaking in their hearts also became true believers. They were faithful to the truth they knew and they expressed true faith in Me.

Then through the ages, many other people heard parts

of the message of Jesus. But it was garbled or truncated, and they didn't receive enough to exercise true faith. However, in many cases they had a single name: Jesus, and they expressed faith in that name. Again, that was enough for Me. They're the true children of God.

Others heard parts of the message, but didn't understand enough to know the details of Jesus' life and death. What they did understand, though, they believed. And again, that was enough. Such faith, small as it is, is enough to redeem and save.

What about those who have heard only negative about Jesus? Perhaps they were raised Muslim or Jewish where fathers and mothers, priests and rabbis and mullahs taught them untruth. Those people could easily have become confused and as a result were unable to express anything close to true faith. But could I not speak to their hearts? Could I not take the truth they did know and arouse faith in that truth? Yes, I could, and I did in many cases. Those people are as much citizens of heaven as others because they have dealt faithfully with the truth they did have and adhered to it.

Now what of those who are in the world today who have never heard: heathen tribes in Africa, Indians in bastions of Hinduism, Chinese under communist rule who have been misled all the days of their lives? These people still have their consciences. They have Me speaking to them in their hearts. If they believe what I reveal to them personally, they are expressing faith and they become the true children of God.

You might ask, but what if conscience fails and My message in their hearts is garbled? How then can they believe?

All of My Creation speaks of Me. The things that have been created demonstrate the need for a Creator. In Creation, you see such beauties as the mighty oak, the superlative weeping willow, the maple, the elm, the ginkgo, the redwood, the teak. You have creatures the world over from the moose to the giraffe, from the rat to the platypus. These marvelous creatures all show something about My nature and those who will study and learn of them will see something in them that speaks of their creator. And of course, you have the infinite variety and beauty of humankind: their ideas, their speech, their manners, their personalities. All these speak of My creative power, My love of beauty and variety, My wisdom and My love. No one who will think about these things can fail to ask, "Where are these things from? Who made them?" And that will lead them to Me, for My Spirit is guiding them to ask those questions and to find the answers that, if they can discover them no where else, will learn them in the depths of their hearts.

That's pretty expansive. So a person doesn't have to believe in Jesus to be redeemed?

There is no other name given in all Creation under heaven by which a person can be saved. Jesus is indeed the way. However, the depth of one's knowledge of Him varies from person to person. What Jesus have they heard of? What Jesus do they have the truth on? How has Jesus been distorted by others' teaching in their lives and so on? These questions must be answered. The truth is that no one knows Jesus well when he first believes. He remains much a mystery until that person can delve into My word and learn of Him. If a person has not heard of Jesus, then My question is, What truth did they hear and what truths did they believe?

You are forgetting something else: My omniscience. If there is a person somewhere out there who is seeking Me, I know of Him and am quite able to get to him the message and truth he needs to believe.

You are forgetting something else: I am just and righteous, and I will deal justly and righteously with every person who has ever existed. All their words, thoughts and deeds will be reviewed. If anything that happened to them was unfair or wrong, it will come out, and they will be repaid. If they were faithful to the truth they had, even the slightest smidgen of it, I will know, and I will reward them for their faithfulness. All these things are in My word and if you read it, you will find them there.

So basically everything is taken care of?

No one will be treated unjustly, unfairly, or unlovingly. All the facts will come to the surface. Everyone in Creation will witness the proceedings and all will agree with the verdict. God will not deal with anyone in less than a just, godly, and holy way. You can be sure that every person will receive "a fair shake" as you yourselves speak of it.

Then we're not saved by faith alone?

You are. But faith is expressed in many ways. One person shows his faith by his refusal to steal even when he is starving. Another expresses faith by telling the whole world about Jesus, like Billy Graham. Both are people of faith, and both are saved by their faith in the truth that they possessed. To him with little truth, little will be required. And he who had much, of him much will be required.

So I'm in trouble then?

Because you've been given much truth?

Yes.

Only if you are unfaithful to it.

How would I be unfaithful?

By repudiating it. By denying you know Me to others. By pretending you know nothing of Me when others are discussing Me, and not speaking up when untruth is shared. By willfully rejecting My truth and doing what you know is sin, and then not repenting of it.

Can a person lose his salvation?

That is a difficult question to answer. Can a person whom I have redeemed and saved be ripped from My hands and given to Satan? No. I will lose none of those I make My own. No one can snatch them out of My hand.

On the other hand, what of a person who supposedly believes at one point in his life and then willfully rejects Me at a later point? The real question is, is it possible for a person who has truly known Me to repudiate Me in the end? Well, Satan knew Me, and he did. A third of the angels knew Me, and they did. Cain knew Me, and he did. Judas Iscariot knew My Son intimately, and he did. When a person chooses to go the roadway of sin, he goes only at great peril to himself.

So what You're saying is that a person who knows You and willfully rejects You can lose his salvation?

What is apostasy? It is when a person who once believed

the truth has corrupted it so that he has become a heretic. This can happen, as it has in many cases, when a man who once preached the truth gets involved with a woman not his wife, commits adultery, and begins justifying all kinds of sin in others because of his own sin. Sometimes he becomes enamored of some new theology or cult and teaches falsehood as a result. Or other sin takes hold of his life, and he ceases to hear the truth any longer because he has hardened his heart. Eventually he leaves the faith. His sin has blinded him to the truth, and he is no longer able to hear My words in his heart. Such a person recrucifies My Son to the cross. He will be held accountable. Apostasy is by its nature denying the faith you once believed. How can you be an apostate if you never believed? It is a denial of terms.

We live in a dangerous world.

Indeed, you do. But not without hospitable forces all around you, protecting and guiding you in My name. It is the valley of the shadow. But My rod and staff are real, and you need not fear evil. The only ones who need fear evil are those who do evil. They fear it because they know it is a means of judgment upon those who sin. Those who live by the sword often die by the sword. It is a law of My world, and it will never change. Evil can reward its servants only with more evil, and all evil can do is destroy; it cannot create; it cannot nurture; it cannot love or build up. If I did not stop evil, it would destroy itself in time because its nature is to do evil to everything around it.

What it sounds like to me is that anyone who goes with You cannot lose.

That is correct. They're on the winning team, the only team that has had a perfect season and will continue to have a perfect season. A season, I might add, that will last for eternity.

Well, I'm tired. I need some sleep. Do You ever sleep?

No.

Good, then You can watch over me.

I always do.

Modern Science

If there's an issue that people claim the Bible is wrong about, it's science. Especially Genesis 1. What were You thinking when You gave Moses that story, if You gave Moses that story? Did he just make it up? And there are other places in Scripture where science has trouble. Miracles, of course, are a biggie. Adam and Eve. The Red Sea. Jesus walking on water. The virgin birth. Too many to count. What gives, Lord? Why are these major mistakes in Your Word if Your Word is supposedly infallible and perfect?

It's a long jump from modern science to major mistakes.

Minor mistakes, whatever. The point is that many people refuse to believe Your Word simply because of its faulty science. Perhaps if these passages weren't included, many more people would have believed.

The Word of God spans the beginning of time and goes through the end of time, at least as far as humanity is concerned. Would you suggest that I begin in the middle?

Most novels do.

> My Word is not a novel. It's the story of human history. I
> include everything a person needs to know to trust Me
> and to believe in My Son. Anyone who gives the Bible an
> honest look will find a book of incredible truth, the very
> truth of God. It possesses the very life of God. I breathed
> into its words My life, and those who touch it touch life,
> real life.

I understand that, I'm just concerned about some of the faulty science.

> What exactly do you think is faulty?

Genesis 1.

> And what is faulty about Genesis 1?

*The whole thing. On the first day, You create light and separate
light from darkness. That's fine. That actually goes along with the
concept of a Big Bang, as our own theorists have conceived it.*

> Let's take that Big Bang. As I understand it, scientists say
> that at one time the universe was reduced to a tiny, com-
> pact nodule of stuff the size of the head of a pin, and this
> thing exploded outwards, releasing all the force and power
> of the known universe. They calculate from the present
> readings on the expansion of the universe when this prob-
> ably happened (perhaps 24 billion years ago). And they
> posit that this is a very accurate calculation, even though
> new papers and findings are written nearly every day con-
> tradicting the theory.

*I agree there are some scientists who agree and others who don't,
but most believe that a Big Bang occurred sometime, even if our
time line is not clear.*

So what you're saying is that though there are serious differences of opinion—opinions that never really existed before the twentieth century—that these opinions must be correct.

Well, perhaps there's room for argument.

Remember one thing: science today in your world changes constantly. New theories and ideas erupt into the mainstream nearly every year. Yet, My Word has stood in the minds of many great scientists of the past for over four thousand years. That's a pretty good track record.

I can agree with that. But why didn't You tell us about the Big Bang?

I said, "In the beginning God created the heavens and the earth." The Big Bang is an attempt to specify what exactly happened. My story is a sketchy list of events that in My mind describe what happened in enough detail to satisfy thousands of years of searching men and women. Remember this: My Word was written to men and women and children who lived in ages and places far removed from modern science. They would not understand the Big Bang and the idea of 24 billion years, even if I told them explicitly. I was not trying to give a scientific paper on Creation in Genesis 1. My purpose was to offer to mankind in many ages and times and places a basic thumbprint idea of what happened at the beginning of the universe. It all had to start somewhere. I planted the curious nature within man. He would inevitably ask the questions. So I satisfied him from the start. I gave him what he needed to understand the beginning of the universe and why things have gone awry.

That makes sense.

Of course it does. Modern man repeatedly makes the mistake of thinking all ages were like his. But at one time people believed the world was flat, even though I told them in Isaiah that the earth was a circle or sphere. People argued back and forth because they could not see how people could stand upright on the sides and bottom of the sphere. They'd be upside down, they reasoned. So until Isaac Newton, who was a stout believer in Genesis 1, no one understood gravity. Even today few pretend to understand how or why it works. They only know that it does. If they would look in the book of Colossians, they would see that I told them through My servant Paul that Jesus "holds all things together." Gravity is the scientific term. My power is the reality. It is My power that holds atoms, amoebas, azaleas, and asteroids in their places. It is my power that makes gravity gravity. But scientists prefer to leave Me out of the equation, so they look for another explanation. To their own peril, I might add.

Okay, but Genesis 1 still has some problems.

Go on.

The fourth day. You create the sun, moon, and stars. Before that, there was only light and darkness. On the third day, You create all the vegetation. So what You're saying is that the sun didn't even exist while vegetation was growing all over earth.

Let's look at this from another angle. Doesn't the basic outline of Genesis 1 reflect the way most scientists conceive of Creation as happening. The order, I mean. First, light. Next space and darkness. After that vegetation. Following that, fish and birds. Finally animals and mankind. The basic outline works, doesn't it?

From an evolutionary perspective, yes, I admit it goes along with that outline, if You believe in evolution.

There are many ideas floating out there about evolution, too. And many scientists who believe that the mechanism— mutations and natural selection—could not possibly have created, through time and chance, the variety and spectacular array of things in Creation. For instance, there's Goldschmidt who posits the idea of the "hopeful monster" in which reptiles suddenly gave birth to birds. Why did he resort to this? Because he found Darwin's explanations for the vast variety and perfection of Creation as it presently exists impossible. So do many others.

Then there's Francis Crick, who was half of the team who discovered DNA, the basic mechanism through which I inscribe all the details of how an organism develops and arranges itself. Crick believes in "panspermia" in which the planet earth was seeded with life forms from life forms from another planet. This, of course, begs the question: where did those other life forms come from? It gets back to the same issue.

Scientists today have discovered much about the order that I have invested in the structure of the universe. They have seen that if the universe expanded one percent faster than it does now, everything would zoom out of control and nothing could be held in place. If it expanded one percent slower than it is now, it would collapse upon itself. Why is it expanding at precisely the right rate? Why is the sun precisely the right distance from the earth to allow for life to exist? Why is the tilt of the earth exactly right to guarantee the seasons of the year and to insure an environment fit for living? Why is the cell, the smallest structure within an organism, so complex, and who makes the mitochondria and the nucleus and all the other elements work together in perfect harmony? What guides cells in producing various organs of the body—the liver, the pancreas, the heart, the lungs? You say DNA. But how does it work? What makes it work? Why does the human eye, and the eyes of so many other creatures function so perfectly? How was it formed through time and chance evolution with natural selection playing a part? No one knows. No one even attempts to show the progression. Why? Because there is no progression. These things came into existence wholly formed, complete and functional. How could that have happened? What made it happen? Are inexorable time and the chancey interlocution of molecules the real answer?

Today, some scientists have come to believe in catastrophism, the idea that certain catastrophes in the weather and in space coincided with the sudden arrival of life forms. Their fossil research demonstrates that life forms appear suddenly in many places. There are few to no "missing links." Where are all the in-between creatures that Darwin suggested they'd find in later times? They haven't been found.

What makes Me angry is this constant effort to leave Me out of it. Why are people so determined that I could not have played a part, in fact, the supreme role? Why do they insist on coming up with a theory that explains everything minus God?

I don't know the answer, Father.

Maybe an illustration will help.

Go ahead.

Two scientists argued about whether God had created the universe or not. One believed God had; the other didn't believe a creator existed at all. They decided to perform an experiment. They purchased a plot of land which they called, "God's Garden," and said, "If God is real, He'll turn this useless plot of ground into a garden." The unbeliever told the believer to pray that God would do this, and he would watch and make calculations.

One morning they woke up to find the rim of the garden ringed with roses of every sort and color. The believer said, "See, God planted the roses. Only He could make them come up overnight."

But the unbeliever said, "No, there is one strain of rose that grows very rapidly. It's simply the process of evolution."

The believer went back to his knees.

The next morning the whole garden was filled with vegetables in rows: corn, potatoes, squash, tomatoes. They were all perfect, larger than life, succulent. The believer said to the unbeliever, "Who could have done this but God?"

The unbeliever shook his head. "Did you see anybody? These aren't unusual vegetables. They only grew quickly. Given enough time and chance the garden could have organized itself this way."

The believer was frustrated but he decided to pray again.

The next morning a giant tree sat in the middle of the garden with a magnificent treehouse at its top. The believer went down and invited his friend to see it. Then he said, "Who else but God could have made such a place?"

But the unbeliever retorted, "If He's here then why

doesn't He join us? Someone probably sneaked in here and did it overnight. My hunch is that an alien did it."

The believer decided to pray at least once more.

The next morning he visited the treehouse and talked with an angel. The believer ran down to get the unbeliever. They climbed up into the treehouse. The angel sat in an easy chair and welcomed them both. But the unbeliever only laughed. "Why it's just a little old man from the village. How much did you pay him to dress up like this?"

The unbeliever left and told all his fellow scientists that his friend had gone mad. They decided to drum him out of the scientific organization.

But the believer sat down with the angel and asked, "When I saw you, I knew you were from God. Only God could have a servant like you. But when he saw you, he said all you were was a little old man. Why?"

The angel smiled. "What did he see when the roses were put at the edge of the garden?"

"Ordinary roses. One more step in the process of evolution."

"And the vegetables?"

"Plain vegetables that grew fast."

"And the treehouse?"

"Just a simple treehouse made by an alien."

"So what did you expect him to see when he saw Me?"

The unbeliever nodded, but said, "But what if God Himself comes down and shows Himself to my friend. Wouldn't he believe then?"

"No," the angel said sadly. "If he didn't believe when he saw the roses or the vegetables or the treehouse or Me, he won't believe when he sees God."

"But why not?"
"Because he doesn't want to."

Interesting.

Yes. Scientists who believe in evolution offer only the sketchiest of details about how human beings came to be. Yet, scientists believe their theory explains everything. In effect, when you get down to the nittiest and grittiest, they are bereft of realistic explanations. They cannot tell you how the human eye, ear, nose, mouth, brain, heart, muscles, or anything came into existence. There is no clear progression from a sensitive nub on the face to the full optical capacity of the eye. Yet, they state their theory as if they'd shown every detail within it. It's nonsense.

This is basic human depravity, the worldview that leaves God out. It is the nature of Satan to offer mankind explanations for the origin of life that leave Me out. It's to his advantage. So, many people believe his little theories. But when you examine them, they break down. Someone has written that for time plus chance to produce even the most basic protein molecule it would take 10 to the 243 billion years. That's ten followed by 243 zeroes, a number that would boggle My mind I suppose if I really thought about it. It's impossible. Yet men persist in believing it.

Despite the surprises in Genesis 1, it is the truth. I created the heavens and the earth. I did it by a process of trial and success, not trial and error. I do not create faulty creatures. I did it over a period of time, which I describe as seven days. Why should I elaborate? Something exists. You have to explain why, or accept My explanation. What else is there? Evolution to the average person seems plausible on the surface, but it's simplistic. It doesn't begin to explain the first trillionth of anything. But people are gullible. They will swallow anything when they're desperate.

Why do You say desperate?

If you accept a Creator who created Creation, then you will soon realize this Creator has revealed Himself. When you move into revelation, you soon arrive at the Bible. It's the most believable explanation of everything out there because it's the right one. As you get into the Bible, you soon discover a God who calls His people to account for their lives. This means they cannot simply do as they please. They answer to Me. People don't like that. They prefer to think they're on their own, they can do whatever they wish, they needn't worry about morals or values or truth. They can just live as they please without a concern for the consequences. Of course Satan will tell them this. "There is no God. Do whatever you want. Don't worry about judgment. Don't worry about Christ. Don't worry about being holy or truthful or righteous. Do your own thing. That's what life is all about."

People pursue this lifestyle thinking it will satisfy them. They support their beliefs with the most hallowed "truths" of all, those of science. If science says it must have happened such a way, then it must have happened that way. Science becomes God. But science doesn't call anyone to account. In fact, science tells them, "It's survival of the fittest. Might makes right. Those who succeed will continue to succeed." This appeals to Americans and Europeans who have so much wealth, freedom, leisure, and everything else. But what about the poor? The hurting? The sick? Eventually, science will tell them to get rid of such people. They're a drag on the evolutionary process. People will clone the beautiful, the smart, the lovely, the physically flawless. It'll be Nazi Germany all over again. And Nazi Germany was only a reflection of every other tyrant who existed before them, going back ultimately to Satan. The god of science leads to tyranny, dissolution, poverty, and spiritual destruction. Yet people embrace it because it pretends to have the facts on its side. But people will perish in their ignorance. As one of your own inventors has said, "We don't know a half percent of a hundredth of a thousandth of anything." You don't know what gravity is. You don't know why light works as both a stream of particles and a wave. You don't know why the earth exists where it does. You don't know who else populates the universe. You don't know why stars are born or why they die. You don't know what it is that makes a deer rut and a fawn stick to its mother. You don't know why cats are like cats and dogs are like dogs. Yes, you have your computers and your VCRs and your TVs. But what do you really have? Just a few playthings. You know very little about anything. And the ignorance of the base population only grows by the day. Illiteracy reigns and one day it will bring you all down.

You paint a sad picture.

Much of what passes for science today, especially theoretical science, plays right into the hands of My enemies. They will do anything to prevent people from coming to Me, from finding Me, from living for Me. If people find an explanation of life that appeals to them, which leaves Me out, they will take it. Unless I do something.

What?

Unless I make them uncomfortable enough to begin seeking Me. And then they will find true life. No true believer finds Creation improbable. If I can part the Red Sea, if I can feed 5,000 men (to say nothing of women and children) with five crackers and three bits of fish, if can heal a leper at a word, if I can still the storm with a mere wave of My hand, if I can raise a dead man who has been dead for four days, if I can raise every person since the beginning of time and make him stand before Me to answer for his life, why couldn't I create a gazelle, or a paramecium, or a frog, or a rose? These things are simple. Creation is easy. I think it, I speak it, and it is. Simple. What is hard though, is conversion. What is difficult is bringing a man or woman out of darkness into light. What is impossible for any human being is opening the heart to the truth. Maybe a story here will help.

Good, another one.

I've got a million.

Imagine Jesus and an evolutionist sitting down before you. You've come to decide whom you'll commit your life to. So you say to Jesus, "If I believe in You, what will I gain?"

Jesus says, "I will give you abundant life." "I'll give you rest." "I'll lead you into all truth and the truth will make you free." "I offer you forgiveness and life forever in My kingdom."

You turn to the evolutionist and say, "And what does your theory offer?"

"Well," he stammers, "every now and then you'll get into a good scientific discussion and argument, and other scientists will respect you."

You turn again to Jesus. "What hope do You offer me?"

He replies, "The hope of heaven and eternal life."

You look at the evolutionist. "And what hope does evolution offer?"

"Only that you'll survive if you're fit, and that you'll eventually die."

You ask Jesus, "What proof is there that You're right?"

He answers, "I have done miracles all throughout history which eyewitnesses have recorded in My Word. I Myself came among men, did miracles, rose from the dead, and started a church which has survived despite persecution, malice, and hatred for centuries. There are millions the world over who can attest to the ways in which I've changed their lives for the better."

You turn again to the evolutionist. "And what proof do you have?"

"Well, there's the fossil record."

"But that's full of gaps."

"We'll straighten that out someday. And there are mutations."

"But not one we've observed has produced a new and different creature."

"Time will tell there. We just don't know enough yet."

You ask him, "And what is the end to which evolution is leading us?"

He replies, "According to the Second Law of thermodynamics, it's all winding down to a huge glob of stuff rolling around at the bottom of the universe."

"What about You, Lord. What is the end of Your theory?"

Jesus answers, "A kingdom of righteousness, holiness, power, and glory forever where God will reign and no evil will ever touch it again."

You ponder a moment and finally you ask, "And what

kind of commitment must I make to your theory, evolutionist?"

Suddenly, the evolutionist perks up. "There's no commitment at all. You don't have to change your life, or do a thing."

You look at Jesus. "And what commitment must I make to You?"

"You must believe, take up your cross and follow Me. You must repent of your sins and seek to lead a holy life by My power."

You stop, ponder, and finally it's your chance to make a decision. What decision do you think you'd make?

I've already made it.

But many haven't. Many won't. Many refuse.

To their own peril.

Correct.

Let's get back to something You were saying before about miracles. It's true that the Biblical miracles are real miracles?

The Bible is the most completely documented and "proved" book in human history. Where archaeology has touched on the truth of the Bible, it has always found it infallible. Where history has impinged on a story or situation in Scripture, it has always demonstrated complete accuracy. There are problems, yes, for humankind. There are things I have not fully explained. There are major events that record only the barest of details. There are difficulties in some texts of times and places. But I have placed within the fabric of human history proof of everything that has ever been and ever will be challenged. Over time people have listed "errors" and problems in Scripture and stated they'd never be overturned. Details about Abraham and Isaac and Jacob. Problems with the fall of Jericho, or the plagues of Egypt. Every few years some local yokel produces a list of difficulties which he says "will never be resolved." Then archaeologists and linguists and scholars and anthropologists go digging and what do they find: proof that the Bible was correct. I have placed these little "corrections" all through the world, and time will show them to everyone. It only takes a little patience.

But why? Why didn't You give us all the proofs up front?

How could I? And why should I? Most people took the stories of Scripture as truth because it was so well documented—until the 19th century. But ultimately, the reason I have done it the way I have is because I am working toward a goal: to build trust. The way you build trust is by allowing a person to test you. When he finds you true, he trusts. Gradually, he begins to trust you about even the things he doesn't understand because so many other things have been proven. It's a relationship. It's worked out day by day. A person prays, I answer. The answer bolsters his faith. It emboldens him to pray some more. I give more answers. His faith grows. He reads My word. He finds a difficulty. I lead him into some texts and books where he finds viable answers. The answers strengthen him. His faith grows some more. That's the way I work. Line by line, brick by brick. Eventually you build a person who is a fortress against error and untruth. That is my goal.

But why do people insist so stridently that the Bible is wrong, even when proofs have come to notice?

It is only the sinfulness of mankind that makes him insist on errors when no errors are there. He is mostly misinformed. But he does not wish to be informed. He prefers his ignorance, for knowledge leads to accountability, and accountability leads to life change, and life change leads to inconvenience and problems and pain and difficulties. People do not want to change. So they will grasp their theories and hold onto them like a child with a shiny new dime. Their only problem is that a dime buys little to nothing in today's market. People who embrace science as god are usually the most miserable of all, for their lack of conviction about moral truth leads them into a moral morass. And that pit is pain personified.

What would You advise a person to do who holds a scientific degree, or believes that science and the Bible conflict?

I would urge him to read My Word. I would tell him to seek Me in prayer with whatever faith he can muster. I will answer. I will give him insight. I will open his mind to the truth, if he will let Me.

So Your most challenging project is always man himself?

Always a challenge, but also a great joy.

What happens when a scientist comes to Christ?

The heavens rejoice. Angels sing. My Son and I kill the fatted calf and have a party.

Too bad for the fatted calf.

I make no apology for My tastes. Cholesterol and fat content make no difference to Me. I don't have arteries. I'm Spirit.

But what about us? Science has discovered that red meat is bad for us?

> Bad for you only in the sense that it may not allow you to live past seventy or eighty.

People have heart attacks in their thirties and forties.

> It's becoming more common. But until the twentieth century, most people didn't live past forty-five. Now the average life span, with all the cholesterol and fat blather going on, is still into the seventies. What makes a man or woman unhealthy is not red meat, but sin. Sin is far more lethal. Sin not only destroys a single life, but families, communities, and nations.

I guess I can agree with that.

> Science has no mechanism for dealing with sin. Even most psychiatrists, who practice the so-called science of the heart and mind, refuse to give credence to the idea of sin. It's always a sickness or illness or an addiction or some other such nonsense. The fact is that sin clogs the arteries and eats up the heart faster than any cholesterol. Nothing makes living good better than morals. But morals can't be lived out in a vacuum. You can't effectively have morals without a ground or source of those morals. Some people try to live good, decent lives, but they have nothing to do with Me. To be sure, I will bless their decency because you reap what you sow. I will not change that law. But in the end, their morals get them nothing but a good, decent, and maybe long life. Morals without God are fool's morals. As one of your prophets has said, "Ministers are paid to be good. The rest of you are good for nothing." The next

world is the true world, and if they have done nothing to prepare for it, they are fools indeed.

Why don't You simply blow us all away with some incredible find like Noah's Ark? What if that was discovered somewhere on Mt. Ararat? Wouldn't that knock the world into sensibility? Wouldn't that produce faith?

If they don't believe My Son and My Word, they won't believe if Noah's Ark was found. You know, that's the problem with miracles. A miracle will move a person in the direction of faith. It may even induce faith. But what happens when new hard times come? What happens when the next disaster doesn't lead to a miracle? If their faith is based on miracles, they have no depth. Faith should not be in what I do, but in Me, in My Son, in who we are. True faith trusts a Person, not a Power because a Person possesses the power and wields the power. When you trust the person, you get the power thrown in. When you trust the power, you can never be sure it will be there when you need it.

What about faith-healers? Are they for real?

The fact is that I do heal. Sometimes I heal in the context of a faith-healing service. But faith-healers possess no power in and of themselves. If I do not act, they can do nothing. At one time, I gave the disciples and the apostles the power to heal at will. Whole districts became healthy at their appearance. Jesus virtually wiped out illness during His three years of ministry in Israel. But I have not given "no-strings-attached" healing power to anyone today. There are many charlatans. There are people who will use the gullibility of those who attend their services to take their money and their faith and use it for their own purposes. But there are also genuine men and women of God in whom I've put a concern and a compassion for the sick and dying. I hear their prayers just like I hear anyone's prayers. And I answer them as simply and directly as I choose. The effective prayer of a righteous person can accomplish great things. People have not tapped into the power of prayer like they once did. They rely too much on their doctors, their lawyers, their accountants, and their technocrats to solve their problems. A man who never learns to pray, fervently and enduringly, is an unhealthy man. I made people dependent creatures. They can do nothing apart from Me. But it takes a long time for them to realize this.

There is power in prayer?

Great power. The whole power of the universe, the whole power of the Mind behind the universe, the whole power of God Himself responds to the smallest child's sincere prayer. I act in response to prayer. When people pray, I move. It's that simple. When people don't pray, I sit back and watch, let them fail and become frustrated. Then they pray as a last resort, and I have to choose whether to reinforce them in their nonpraying attitude by doing what they ask, or I must say, no, I want to see some fervor here, some fire. I am not a bailout artist. I'm not a soda machine, where you put in your prayer and you get your product. People need to grow into prayer as a lifestyle. When prayer becomes part of the fabric of a man's life, it's then that My true power is unleashed. Some churches today exist and flourish because of the exuberant and enduring prayers of one or two of my warriors. A battle can be more successfully fought on one's knees than with guns and tanks. Americans, in particular, need to learn this.

Should we pray about the problems in Iraq, about the problems in Israel with the Palestinians?

About everything. Pray without ceasing. Never let up. Never let Me off the hook. I love a person who debates, who comes to Me with reasonable reasons, who negotiates, who tries to persuade Me of some action. Many people feel they should simply name their request and I'll either answer or I'll not answer. They have no fire, no passion. I am easily moved by a person who "feels" their need, who takes care with the words they bring to Me, who studies My Word to see whether what they request is something that goes along with My will. People treat prayer as a "try-it-and-see" kind of mechanism. They'll try it for now, but if it doesn't work, do something else. No, I say, keep praying. Don't faint. Don't give in. Refuse to let Me tell you no if it's something you're committed to. Keep coming back to the throne room and asking for My audience. I often grant a request only after its been poked at and thought about for months and even years. I loathe the passionlessness I see in My people. They don't want to "show any emotion." I say, prove to Me that you need this. Show Me with your words, your actions, your heart that this is something you hunger for. I respond to hearts that hunger.

Yet, there are times when You don't answer a person for years, sometimes never. Like a person who prays for healing. Like that young policeman who committed suicide. Why didn't You answer them?

I did answer them.

With a no?

> In some cases. In other cases, I showed them that I had something else in mind. Paul entreated Me three times to take the thorn of Satan out of his flesh. I said no, for My power is made perfect in weakness. Paul's weakness and his commitment to succeeding despite his weakness led to ends I felt were better than merely relieving him of his pain. Pain is not a bad thing. With it, I get a person's attention. People in pain are some of the most fervent prayers you will ever see in this world. Pain drives men and women to God. Therefore, I see it as a good thing, not something to be taken away immediately, and in some cases, not ever. That's the problem of science. It often relieves a person of the consequences of their sin—pain, disease, trouble—that I have sent them to wake them up. At one time, syphilis was a disease passed on through sinful people taking sinful advantage of other sinful people. Science discovered penicillin, which kills syphilis. Presto, no more problem. Go sin again, and if you catch a disease, get a hypodermic shot. Nothing to worry about. What they don't see is that there are more consequences to such sin than simply the disease. And those consequences are far more severe, far more painful, than anything the disease could produce. Science only gets at the surface of things. It cannot fix the basic problem of the human heart and soul.

We always come back to that.

> It's the most basic issue of all. Until it's settled, nothing's settled.

I'm glad I've settled it.

You and Me both.

Just how glad are You?

I killed the fatted calf, had some terrific brisket.

Next time invite me.

Oh, you had your own feast all right, as I recall.

(I laugh.) Yes, I guess I did. I want to come back to these things, Father.

We will.

I guess You know.

I knew it all before the first particle of life was set in motion.

So You're a know-it-all?

The only true one.

Then You know what I'm going to say next.

Of course.

What?

"I wish I could lay down and go to sleep."

You do?

No, that's what you're planning on saying next.

Oh. Sorry about that. I'm not bored. I'm just . . .

Plumb tuckered out?

Yeah.

Go take a nap. Get some fatted calf. And don't worry about your cholesterol count. Just start eating some fruits and vegetables regularly and things will take care of themselves.

You know, huh?

From before you were born.

All right, I'll be back.

Arrivederci.

Meaning Of Life

Sometimes I wonder, Lord, what exactly is the meaning of life?

Do you mean the purpose of life? Or do you mean what gives a person meaning in life, a sense of destiny, a feeling that you're part of something vaster, bigger than yourself, an inner awareness that you're an important piece of the puzzle or fabric that is the true end and reality of the universe?

Both, I suppose.

Let's take the second one first. The thing that gives a person that kind of meaning and purposefulness is, one, personally knowing his Creator and Lord and having a relationship with Him that involves the full spectrum of human emotion; second, living out what that creator fashioned and designed him to be; and third, knowing that he is living out that design and therefore fitting into the vast puzzle of life in an important and even, in a sense, indispensable way. Without a belief that he is important to Me and a relationship with Me is necessary, he will flounder about always feeling disconnected and that there's no one in his life who truly understands him. Without involving himself in the lifestyle, work, and opportunities of life for which I designed him, he will feel useless (in some cases) or driven (in others). He will never feel truly a part of the great drama that is Creation, but always be a person standing off in the wings wishing he could play a role and not only receive a bit of the applause but also have an impact on the lives and fortunes of others.

This is getting complicated.

Of course, but it's really quite simple. Maybe a parable will help.

Parable?

You recall I often spoke in parables.

Yes, but . . .

I still do. Here's a new one. The Creator wanted to create the greatest baseball team ever.

Baseball team?

I'm a fan. (Chuckles.) Hey, who do you think gave the original baseball player the idea anyway?

(I smile.) It's an image I can't quite grasp.

If people accused Me of being a glutton and a drunkard in the first century because I happened to enjoy eating and drinking (without getting drunk, of course), don't you think I also might enjoy a ball game now and then? And a Ball Park hot dog with mustard, Nacho chips with cheese, and a fizzy soda or Orange Julius?

I guess.

Don't guess. Accept. Believe. Enjoy.

On with the parable.

Of course. The Creator puts together this fantastic ball team. He's got DiMaggio in left field, Babe Ruth at first, Hank Aaron as designated hitter—I go with the AL rules on that one—Cal Ripken at short, Brooks Robinson at third, the whole incredible lineup, Johnny Bench catching, and Bill McGoogle on the mound.

Bill McGoogle?

You'd prefer Nolan Ryan?

Well, no, but . . .

Christy Matthewson?

Maybe, but . . .

Whitey Ford?

It's just that I don't think I've ever heard of Bill WhatsHisBucket?

Well, now you have. I'm the creator. I create, all right?

Go for it.

Now imagine that I've designed each of these players for their particular positions and abilities. I've given them those abilities as well as the commitment and gumption to make the most of them. But suppose Bill McDoogle . . .

McGoogle.

Right. Just making sure you're listening. Suppose this Bill

McGoogle fellow gets out there on the mound and he pitches, pitches so well in fact that it's a shutout. Two hits, no runs, fourteen strikeouts. A great day. Howard Cosell is interviewing him . . .

He's not around anymore.

Only in your time frame. In mine, he's there all the time.

Okay.

Laugh a little, son. Don't take things so seriously.

I'm trying.

This McGoogle is being interviewed, lots of attention, the whole shebang, and he's feeling quite good about it. He's being what he was meant to be. That season he pitches well, ends up 22-7, a good record, thinks he's a shoo-in for the Cy Young. He goes on into the World Series, pitches wonderfully, wins MVP and so on, and does win the Cy Young in the end. This goes on for several years. He's got the multi-million dollar contracts, he's riding a wave of applause, but eventually he's had his time in the limelight, and he fades. Now, all along I've known this was coming, and I was prepared for it. I have invested his life with certain other qualities and abilities that, when tapped, will continue to give him a sense of destiny and fulfillment, though perhaps not in the public eye as he has been. At any rate, the time comes when he begins to notice that it's the coach, Me the Creator, who has put him there. And it's the coach who's telling him what to pitch. And it's the coach who continues on for years while McGoogle fades away. Fans boo him. He's not getting the acclaim he thinks he deserves. Sports writers pan him as a has-been.

So one day, McGoogle's out there on the mound muttering about his lousy lot in life, and he gets into trouble in the fifth inning. I, the coach, stalk out to mound. "Tough time today, huh, Bill?"

"Yeah," Bill answers. "But I've still got the oil."

"I disagree," the coach says. "I think the well is dry. Go in and take a shower."

"It's not," Bill says. "I can pull it off."

"No, I'm pulling you off the mound."

As the coach walks back to the dugout, McGoogle suddenly decides all his trouble is the coach's fault. So he gets an idea: he won't throw pitches to the plate; he'll throw them at the coach. After all, it's the coach who made him get out here and pitch in the first place. It's the coach who has humiliated him in front of 50,000 fans. (I could give you an exact count, if you want). It's the coach who has failed to see McGoogle's real talent. So nail the coach!

He starts throwing balls at the coach. Meanwhile, some of the other players are disgruntled too, and they join in. Soon, you've got half the team waling on the coach. And why? Basically because one person stopped believing that the coach had his best interest at heart. Basically because one person doesn't think the coach knows what he's doing.

Just as baseball players must listen to the coach to learn the best way to fit into the ball game, so men and women must gain their purpose by listening to Me and walking in the path I have laid out for them. The difference between Myself and a human coach is that a coach is fallible, imperfect, stuck in the same time frame as everyone else. I on the other hand know the end from the beginning. I shaped that player. I wove him together in his mother's womb. I put each quality he would need into his muscles and into his psyche and into his personality. I even gave him the strength to put in the discipline he'd need to achieve his goals.

Moreover, I know where he's going. I know how he fits into the ultimate game plan, the plan that shapes all of human history. He can't see that, except what I've revealed in scripture. So he has to trust Me to get him to where he wants to go. He has to believe that I have his best interest at heart, for I do. He must look to Me day by day for the outworking of that wonderful plan. Only then will he find himself fitting into it and reaping the fulfillment that I came to give him.

Does that mean we can't disagree?

Of course not. You can disagree, voice your opinion, say what's on your mind. And maybe you'll change the coach's mind about what he plans to do. That's the essence of prayer. Prayer is telling Me what you desire and influencing Me to go in a certain direction. I have changed a situation, transformed an event of history many times because My people prayed. I work in response to prayer, just as I Myself have put it into My people to pray when the time is right.

But how do we find this meaning? How do we discover our purpose?

It comes out as part of the process of relating to Me, knowing Me, walking with Me day by day, year by year. It's a moment by moment process. You see, the purpose and meaning of life is not static. It's not this "one great meaning" and that's it. There are many purposes. There are also times when one purpose is no longer a priority or even a reality. It's pushed aside to make room for a second purpose. Later that second purpose dies and a third is found. In a lifetime, a believer may find himself in many occupations, several lifestyles, and many smaller periods of time where the thing that once drove and compelled him has lost its glow. Just like Bill McGoogle found fulfillment in being a pitcher during his early adult years, he would also find that eventually he could no longer perform in that arena. So he would leave his pitching behind and find a new purpose that I, as his coach, would show him were he to continue to talk to Me about it. The ultimate goal of every one of My people is to keep depending on the coach, keep trusting the coach, and he will lead you in the straight way.

Like that verse in Proverbs.

Precisely. "Trust in Me with all your heart and do not take your own perception of things as the final answer; in all your ways look to Me for the true answer, and I will lead you in the straight and fulfilling way."

If the meaning of life then, is to trust You and rely on You to show me the path, then it's crucial that I relate to You on a daily basis.

Absolutely. The only real meaning that lasts is the meaning that comes through your knowing that you are pleasing Me. It's like a child with her father. When she knows she has pleased him, she is happiest. When she sees the light in his eyes and the smile on his lips, she is carried along on an internal breeze of joy and inspiration. She is pleased when he is pleased. Her pleasure is wrapped up in his pleasure. On the other hand, when she knows she has displeased him, she feels guilty and mopes, or responds with anger and even hatred. She feels empty, bitter, displaced, upset. Things aren't right and they're not right because she knows she has displeased him. But if she repents and returns, her father accepts her and assures her of his love, and then takes her by the hands and shows her what he wishes her to do.

That sounds a bit autocratic to me.

In a way. But that is the way I have constructed humanity. Every human has a longing to be loved, accepted, cared for, listened to. For every human, there are many others I have placed in their lives who can do some of these things. When I created Adam, I saw that he in fact needed more than just Me to be fulfilled. So I gave him Eve. Adam could have been happy relating only to me and to his work. But I knew he needed "one like himself," a helpmate who would complete him, take him beyond his limited world and outlook and see the full breadth of the picture. I alone can fulfill the deepest needs of the human heart: the need for meaning, purpose, peace, character, hope, life, understanding, and unconditional love. No other human can provide those realities.

And that is why it is so crucial that each person come into a friendly, open and reverent relationship with Me. Only then will he or she be truly fulfilled. It's the way I made you.

But why can't it be some other way?

There is another way: Satan's. That is the way of rebellion, malice, hatred, murder, strife, jealousy, brokenness, and all the other negative emotions and acts that go with a lifestyle that wants nothing to do with Me. That is the way most of the world has gone since the sin in the Garden of Eden. Throughout human history, I have prevented the world from falling into complete and utter degradation. I have always raised up a remnant who would become salt and light to the rest. But that remnant always had a choice. Every person has the freedom and right to decide whether they wish to know and relate to Me, or reject and hate Me. I will not force Myself on anyone. However, when you choose Satan's way, you also must accept the problems, the consequences, that go with it: meaninglessness, hopelessness, desperation, tyranny, division, and general malice toward all. It's a law as imbedded in the universe as gravity.

If this is so, then why don't more people come to You, follow You, love You?

Humankind is a stubborn race. They want to try their own way first before submitting to what they assume will be slavery. Of course, what they don't realize is that running from Me is the real slavery, and walking with Me is the only true freedom. The truth, "You shall have life and shall have it abundantly," is only possible when you are linked spiritually, mentally, and emotionally to the giver and creator of life.

So if I want real meaning and purpose I must come to You, embrace You, love You? It sounds so one-sided.

Believe Me, it is not. I sent Jesus to the cross to make it possible for you to know Me and be with Me all your days. The payment I made was My way of telling you how much I was willing to sacrifice for you, that you might live and find fulfillment and freedom. What greater love is there than a person who is willing to die in order that others might live? That is what I did because I love you and have always loved you. It was not an easy price to pay. Jesus in fact flinched from it. He asked Me to let that cup pass. I chose not to, and He chose to obey. At any point He could have cried Uncle, and I would not have made Him go to the cross. But I knew if He didn't, the world, life, people, you yourself, could never have existed. I would have been forced to destroy it all the moment Adam sinned. Jesus paid the price of personal torture, pain, and damnation on that cross because I saw something greater, something infinitely more worthwhile than His own pleasure and preference. That thing I saw was you, your family, your neighbors, your loved ones, and those of every generation of mankind with Me in heaven forever. When I saw you and all of yours, I knew I could pay the price without looking back. I have no regrets, except that so many refuse to believe I love them and wish only the best for their lives and their destinies.

But you must also understand one other thing: those who come to Me and love Me will soon find that I will give them much in return, far more than they could ever think to gain on their own. I offer you eternal life, a home in heaven, eternal friendship, an education plan that is out of this world, pleasures and opportunities you can barely begin to conceive, an inheritance that would put any ERP to shame, a friendship that will go on and on forever on ever greater waves of love and devotion, and I offer it all for free. All you have to do is say, "I will follow You." That's all I ask. What I'm asking really is, "Will you come and share with Me all that I own and have?" Who would turn down the opportunity to be ERP's heir? Yet, I'm offering you much more, to be My heir, My friend, My lover, and to be that forever.

It's My greatest pain and agony that My people, whom I love, whom I died for, think I'm nothing more than a cardboard dictator, a cosmic killjoy, a coward, and a traitor to all that is good and worthwhile and perfect. That is the lie My enemy Satan tells people everyday, and it's My sad but determined duty to mine it out of people and show them the true gold of My care.

You sound like a jilted lover.

In some ways, I am. But I am content to know that many millions remain My best friends and closest confidants, and for Me that is encouragement enough to endure the onslaught of lies.

Why are there so many lies about You?

When I've got all the truth on My side, what else is there?

I like knowing You, Lord.

And I you.

Let's have a bite to eat.

Your place or mine?

Yours. I hear the banana splits up there are out of this world.

You should try the Belgian Chocolate Chocolate.

Out of the next world?

You got it.

All Those Religions

Father, something that troubles me is all these religions. Some say they're all true. Some say only one can be true. What's the truth?

Think about it. Buddhism and Hinduism say our goal is Nirvana. You die and live again repeatedly until you get there. Christianity says you die once and after that comes judgment. Both can't possibly be true.

Right. That's the problem.

Islam says Mohammed was God's prophet, His last prophet. He gave his followers the Koran. They believe it's the holiest of books. It was written in the 600s A.D. The Bible says it's the Word of God, and in the end, it says anyone who adds to it will be judged with the plagues in the book. The Koran in that respect is adding to the Word of God. Who's right?

That's what I'm wondering.

Confucianism is a series of principles. Hinduism speaks of the Law of Karma, which means you pay for in your present life what you did wrong in your previous life. The Bible, though, speaks of grace, and forgiveness, and the fact that people suffer because it's an opportunity for God to work in them. Which one is the truth? They can't both be true.

Correct. That's the problem. Some people say there are many ways to God, and each one is a valid way.

Why would I make many ways? Why not one, simple, all-encompassing way to Me? What would be the point of developing different ways that all contradict each other?

No point, I suppose.

It's a matter of making sense. One way makes sense. Truth makes sense. It's the lies of people and the devil that don't make sense when you push them to their limits.

Maybe You can give me an example.

Of course. Here's a story that might illustrate what I'm talking about.

How Holmes had gotten into the pit he didn't know. He'd been there ever since he could remember.

It wasn't such a bad place. Jagged crags jutted up above him. The sun shone down. Sometimes it was unbearably hot. But it wasn't too unpleasant.

He'd tried to climb out many times. But it was impossible. The sides of the pit cut your hands and feet. Where you could get a fingerhold, you were as likely to lose a fingertip as to hold on. Climbing out wasn't the way.

But Holmes wanted out. He hated the pit. It was desolate, lonely. Something within him cried that life had to be better than this.

Then one day a man appeared on the edge of the pit. He looked down and spied Holmes instantly. "So you're in the pit?" he said.

"What's it look like?" answered Holmes cheerlessly. "You know a way out?"

The man nodded. "I'm not sure, but I think the truths of the Buddha may help you get out."

Holmes became excited. "What do I do? Tell me."

The man said, "You must overcome all desire. Follow the eight-fold path and you will break the endless cycle of Karma. Your soul will be set free and you'll be out of the pit, even though your body will still be in it."

Holmes slit his eyes. "My soul will be set free but my body still will be here? What kind of nonsense is that?"

"No nonsense. Just meditate. Then your suffering will end." The man turned to leave.

Holmes snorted. "I guess I can't lose anything trying this." He plopped himself down and tried to clear his mind. "I will think of nothing, do nothing, be nothing," he said. He concentrated. But as he did, it seemed his desire to escape the pit only magnified. After several hours of struggle and failure, he gave up. At that moment, he spotted another man passing by the edge of the pit.

"Hey!" yelled Holmes. "You have any ideas about how to get out of the pit?"

The fellow was wearing a yellow robe and appeared to be bald. "Of course. All you have to do is chant this little chant. Hare Krishna, Hare Krishna, Hare Rama, Hare Rama. Just say it about three thousand times a day."

"Why?"

"It'll make you happy."

Holmes slumped. "I don't want to be happy. I want to be out of the pit."

The fellow yawned. "Sorry. Our book doesn't say anything about pits. Just about how to be happy." He wandered off and Holmes once again was alone.

"Creep!" he shouted. "Creep!"

Suddenly a bearded man with a notebook stopped and gazed at the hapless Holmes. "Can I offer you my services?"

"Who are you?"

"A scientist," he said. "And a doctor of engineering."

"Fantastic!" said Holmes. "Can you engineer a way for me to get out of the pit?"

The scientist looked around. "I think so. I've built such contraptions before. Let me see what I can do."

The scientist brought in a team of students who began putting together a marvelous piece of machinery. In no time the scientist had dropped it in by parachute with a full manual and list of instructions.

"How do I work it?" shouted Holmes.

"Read the directions," said the scientist, and headed off down the road.

Holmes read. And read. And read. He tried this button and that lever. But nothing happened. Then he found the electrical cable.

"There's nowhere down here to plug it in!" he cried.

Holmes shouted again, but his voice only echoed. "Great!" he said. "Now I'm not only not out of the pit, but things are more cluttered up than ever."

He sat down and banged his fist on the ground. "I'll never get out of here."

"I can help," said a smooth voice. A man with a vast smile appeared on the edge of the pit. "If you think you can, you can!" said the man.

"What do you mean by that?" Holmes was intrigued. The man spoke but his smile didn't move at all.

"You must think in terms of possibilities, for all things are possible to him who thinks he can."

"What's the possibility of me getting out of the pit?"

"Just decide in your mind that you can do it," said the smiling figure, "and you'll do it."

"So what do I do now?" asked Holmes.

The man smiled vastly. "Plan. If you fail to plan, you plan to fail. But if you plan to win, your plan will win!"

Holmes felt a bit frustrated. "Will you please speak

English?"

"Plan your work and work your plan," said the man again.

"I don't have a plan," shouted Holmes. "And nothing has worked."

"Tut, tut," the man said. "Just change your thinking, and your thinking will be changed."

Holmes interrupted. "Look, my problem isn't thinking. It's the pit. I want to get out of it."

The man threw him a book, *Success Unlimited*, and said, "You can get other books at the bookstore."

Holmes shouted, "I can't get to the bookstore." But the fellow was gone.

He stomped about in the bottom of the pit, pounding his fist into his palm, and muttering. Then another man appeared on the edge of the pit. He peered down and Holmes was about to speak, but then the man simply clambered over the edge of the pit and begin climbing down. Holmes watched with fascination.

The man found handholds and footholds where there had been sheer rock before. As he drew nearer, Holmes noticed his back, bent and torn. And his hands and feet had great scars on them.

"He must be used to climbing into pits," Holmes said to himself.

It was only minutes until the man alighted and stood before him. "Get on my back," he said.

Holmes was about to protest, but the man's face was so utterly sincere that the hesitation and fear left him. He jumped onto his back.

The man began climbing. Holmes marveled as he watched him pick his way upward. He climbed smoothly, effortlessly from Holmes' point of view, but many times the man cried out in pain. When they reached the top, his fingertips were bloody.

But that wasn't the end. Soon Holmes saw his little pit was in an even deeper pit that the Buddhist, scientist, and others had been. The man began climbing out of this larger pit. The going was rough. But soon they were out.

Holmes hopped off and said with care, "Can I bandage your wounds?" The man held out his hands and Holmes made a dressing from some fresh grass and leaves. When he finished, the joy of being out of the pit struck him. He stood to suck in the cool air. "I can't believe it—I'm out. It was that simple. How can I ever thank you?"

"Just say it," the man said.

Holmes laughed. "That's all? Just say 'Thank you?'"

The man smiled and nodded.

Holmes bowed. "Thank you." He paused. "But how can I ever repay you?"

The man smiled again. "You can't."

Holmes was shocked at this blunt honesty. But suddenly he understood.

"That's strange to say. But you're right. I can't repay you. I can only thank you."

Holmes gazed at the man, perplexed. It had been so simple, so matter-of-fact. He said, "But why did you do this? Why did you come down to get me?"

"Because I love you."

Holmes shook his head. "I don't understand."

"You will." The man got up and began walking away.

Holmes ran after him. "Wait, where are you going?"

"There are other pits, other people."

"But what should I do?"

The man turned, his eyes piercing Holmes to the soul.

"Follow me."

When he said it, Holmes's heart jumped. He stood there momentarily staring back at the pit and the vast landscape before him. "I could just go my own way," he muttered. "Why should I follow him?"

But something within him told him there was much more to this than just being free. "I've got to find out more about this man," Holmes said to himself. He joined the man at his side. "What's your name?"

"I am who I am," he said. "But you may call me 'Lord.'"

Holmes nodded and peered about the countryside around him. He looked into the Lord's eyes and his mind seemed to fill with enormous thoughts, too great to contain. His heart swelled within him.

"This can't be," he said. "I must be half crazy. I'm beginning to think you're much more than a person who climbs down into pits."

"I am."

"But who are you?"

"I am the bread of life, the resurrection, the way, and the truth. But you can't understand all this now. You have to grow."

Holmes bowed before him. "I will follow you. But what do I do?"

Suddenly a cry pierced the air. "Help, I'm in the pit!"

Holmes thought a moment. Suddenly, he leaped. "That's it, Lord! I'll look for people in pits and you can come to rescue them."

The Lord laughed and motioned with his arm. "Do it."

Holmes ran in the direction of the voice. In only moments he found a man in a pit much like his own. He shouted to the man that help was coming. Then he looked toward the Lord and cried, "Over here Lord. This guy is really desperate."

I like that one.

Do you understand what I'm saying?

That all other religions tell us how to get out of the pit of sin and guilt but they never succeed. Man's efforts always fail. But Jesus comes down into the pit of our despair and takes us out of it.

That's right.

So Jesus is the only way?

He's the only one who can go down into pits and pull people out. All the others tell people things they should do to get out of the pit, and they all fail.

Then I will trust Him.

That's what it's all about.

Personal Problems

FRIENDS, ENEMIES,
AND EVERYONE ELSE

Problem

Lord, I know we have this relationship now and it's been great and all that but I just wondered if You knew about . . . about . . .

The problem?

Yes, "the" problem. You know all about it, I guess.

Yes.

I . . . I don't know what to say. I feel so . . . so . . . guilty. Please say something now, Father, because this is not easy.

I understand.

No You don't. You can't. You're perfect, and I'm . . . not.

That does not mean I can't understand. I have also been

tempted through My people. I know what they have felt at every turn. I have walked with them through it in triumph, and in tragedy. I know what it's like to writhe and try to throw a temptation off until you finally give in and gain partial relief. And then the guilt comes, taking the relief away. I think I understand how you feel.

But I have had this problem for . . .

Years.

Yes. For years.

I know all about it.

And You still love me?

Yes.

But why?

Because I love you now, have always loved you, and will always love you. My love will see you through.

But why can't I beat it, Father? Why does it continue to track me day in and day out? I feel like such a failure. Surely it makes You angry.

All sin makes Me angry. But that does not mean I hate you, or that I'd want to hurt you, or punish you. I see it as a difficulty to be overcome. One day soon you will win. Once, twice. Then you'll win again. You'll taste the victory, and you will be strengthened by the times you have won. And perhaps with time and effort it will all fade into the past as a forgotten problem that you battled and overcame. By that time another problem will have come to prominence, and you will do battle there. All of life is a struggle. In this world there are few easy victories. I did not make people to be marshmallows. It takes strong medicine to defeat a strong sickness. Through struggle I make people strong.

But what if I give in next time, and next time, and next time? What if I don't see the victory for a long time?

Then I will forgive you each time and we will go on, determined to do better even if we do not.

We?

We.

Are You sure You don't want to give up on me?

Never, never would I do that. We are husband and wife, father and son, teacher and disciple, creator and creature. Such relationships cannot be broken by mere sin. I have paid for it all.

I promise I'll try, Father.

And I will be with you. Together there is power. One plus Me is a majority.

I trust You, Father.

Good. Hang in there.

Hang in there?

I occasionally use some of your expressions.

Thanks, Father.

My pleasure.

Troublous Person

There's this person, Father. You know who I mean?

Yes.

I don't know what to do. I've tried everything. Nothing works.

Sometimes it is that way.

But I wish things were better.

So do I.

You mean, You can't do anything about it?

I am working on it. But when it comes to human beings, I find that they are very independent. Of course, I could crush her.

No, I wouldn't recommend that.

Neither would I.

Is there anything else You can do?

Much. Speak the truth in love. Confront. Gently lead her in a new direction. Talk to her through her conscience. Send friends who can encourage her and possibly rebuke her, if necessary. Engineer circumstances. Bring her to the end of herself. Have her bottom out. Many things.

So there is hope?

Always.

Then why does it all look so hopeless?

Because you are in the midst of it. I see the end from the

beginning and know where it's all headed. You are burdened by emotions and fears and worries that sap your energy and make you (at times) feel hopeless. There is always hope to him who believes.

So I shouldn't give up?

No.

Is there ever a point of giving up?

In different levels.

What levels?

You can break a relationship that has gone sour and recognize you must each go your own way. You can only make peace if both parties choose to make peace. You can agree to disagree and go on, rarely crossing one another's paths, but when you do remain cordial and tolerant. You can give a person over to their own desires and allow them to go through trouble that will ultimately turn them back. You can give over a person to the power of evil in hopes that the agony of the evil will bring them to repentance. And there is the giving over unto death.

What is that?

That is when a person is so hardened in their course that you recognize only death will free them from the destruction they are experiencing.

When does that take place?

Only at My discretion. It is not for you to decide.

That's a relief.

Indeed.

Well, Father, is there anything else You want to tell me about this?

Do not grow weary of doing good.

I'll try.

Don't just try. Do.

Yes, I will . . .

Good.

Depression Relieved

Tonight I was so depressed, Father. I got into bed with a heavy heart. Forlorn. Fearful. Anxious. Then I picked up a book by a bestselling author. I read it not looking for encouragement but hoping to spot flaws. I wanted to find all the ways I know better than he. But then I got interested. His words calmed me. He was eloquent. Brief. Powerful. Evocative. I could envision the pictures he drew. I was touched. I forgot about my depression. My mind roved over his insights. My spirit was carried aloft on the wind of his words. Now I am writing, thinking, wishing to write as well as he. The clock ticks behind me. The cat naps. It is near midnight. I feel You here, Father. I have felt You speaking to me through this author. And I believe I can make it now, Father. You and me. And the rest of us. We're going to do just fine, aren't we, Father? Aren't we?

Yes.

So You're listening?

I always am.

Sometimes it's hard, Father.

What is hard?

Life. You know.

Your life is not too hard. Just hard enough that turning to Me is easier.

Easier?

There was a time when you would never turn to Me, or think of Me as anything but a bother.

I know. I'm sorry.

No need. That's the way it is. All humans start out on the wrong side of the equation. I draw them. Soon they learn to trust Me. Moses did. So did David. But they didn't start out that way.

I've read their stories.

Then you know.

Does it ever get easier?

It's like a climb through the mountains. Some crags are easy. Some are hard. But the true adventurer presses on into the depths of the mountains. And there he is always challenged.

So it doesn't get easier?

Easier to trust Me for some things. Harder for the things of today.

I don't get it.

Think of it this way. As you grow, you learn to conquer bad habits, nagging sins, flaws of character. Eventually, you move on. You've conquered those things. New problems come into your life. Some you conquer with ease. Others are more difficult. I'm always sending you a mix.

Sending me?

I have ordered your life so that you can continually grow and transform into My likeness.

I've heard that. But I guess I didn't really . . .

Believe it?

Yes.

It's true. I have planned out every day, every moment for you to grow, learn, build spiritual muscles. Don't you know Paul's word to the Ephesians—chapter two, verse ten?

Well, I haven't . . .

Look it up. Memorize it.

Yeah, I guess I should.

Guess?

Well, Father, it's something that I know I should do, but . . .

All right, I won't nag you about it. You'll have to grow into it. Anyway, Ephesians 2:10 says that you are My workmanship, created in Christ Jesus for good works, which I prepared beforehand, that you might walk in them.

Maybe You can explain it.

I have planned out your life so that everyday you have

opportunities to do good. It's My intention that you'll do the good when the opportunity presents itself.

Like me reading that book last night?

Exactly.

How many of these opportunities do You give the average person?

Scores every day. From morning to night.

That many?

Yes.

How come?

So at the end, it'll be plain as day who's the real thing and who isn't.

You mean, the judgment.

Yes.

But what does all this say about human freedom, Father?

You're still free to do as you please.

But if You're sending us all these opportunities . . .

I want you to have some fun. It's My way of making life an adventure. Everyday—new things to do, new people to help, new words to speak to friends and relatives. Everyday chock full of good.

I guess it's a good idea.

Have you thought of what life would be like without such planning?

Chaos?

> Precisely. I am not a creator of chaos.

I promise to memorize that verse, Father.

> I'll test you on it.

Death

What about death, Father?

> It is the last enemy.

But why does it exist?

> You know the story of the Garden. Adam and Eve were warned. They chose the way of death when they ate the fruit of the tree of the knowledge of good and evil. Death is a consequence of sin.

Yes, but isn't there another way?

> In Christ, there is life, eternal life. You will never die the second death.

The second death?

> After the judgment, some will pay for their sins through permanent separation from Me. That is the second death.

But in Christ is life?

> Yes.

Is there anything good about death, Father?

> Of course. I can bring good out of everything that is bad. It

is My way and My grace. I love to turn a bad situation into something good every time.

What good is it, then?

For one thing, it warns us. It tells us that the end is coming and we will face God afterwards. We need to get ready.

I'm not sure I understand.

Let Me tell you a story.

David Leene bent over the books once again. "I can't believe it," he murmured. "Our profits are up 300% in less than a year."

Ah, a story about a real person.

No, I made him up. But he is very real, just the same.

David Leene had already checked his books through twice. When his accountant first rushed in to inform him, he was skeptical. But now he was convinced. "There's no question what I'll do now," he said to himself. "It'll be four more franchises in PA, and one each in NJ, MD, and DC." He reflected on his unique way of referring to the states of his homeland. One of the little trademarks he was known for in the business.

He had a multitude of such idiosyncrasies. The cigar trick was his best. After concluding a big deal, he'd take the corporate brass out to a restaurant, throw a rich repast, and finally pass out thick Cuban stogies wrapped in twenty dollar bills. Then he'd stand and say, "You can keep the twenty if you want, gentleman, but my preference is that you use it to light this delicate little instrument of pleasure. The reason is because once you install my equipment in your factories, you'll soon be lighting up hundred dollar bills."

David Leene laid back in his chair and laughed. "I ought to retire," he mused. "That would be the greatest heist of all. I can see the headlines. 'Leene retires after a 300% year.' I have to take my ease sometime. Do some feasting."

As Leene mused, he became drowsy. His eyelids sagged. In moments he was snoring in the leather burgundy-dyed chair.

Suddenly a sharp sound penetrated his sleep and he jolted awake. After glancing around, he noticed a strange shadow appeared from behind the curtains and Leene's heart jumped. "Who's there?" he said.

To his alarm a voice answered. "I'm sorry. I wanted to get you while you were still asleep."

Leene jumped up and pulled open a drawer, grasping a pistol. "Who are you?" Leene cried, now frightened and white.

"Death," said the voice, quavery and crackly.

Ooooh, this is a horror story.

Indeed.

Leene laughed nervously. "Death! This has got to be a dream."

The shadow moved closer. "I'm sorry, I had planned to get you while still asleep. I really hate these arguments, you know."

Leene swallowed. "You mean this is real?"

The shadow moved as though a head were shaking. "I prefer to get them while they're asleep. Most people complain profusely about it, making threats, screaming. Anyway, I wish I could wait, but I have to begin the count now or I'll be late. Ten, nine . . ."

Leene backed up as the shadow moved forward. "What are you doing? What do you mean 'count'? Am

I about to die?"

"Yes. Eight, seven . . ."

"Hold it!" shouted Leene. "Look, I don't know what you're doing, but I think I ought to at least have an explanation."

Death sighed. "It's the way these things are carried out. I simply count you out. You see, I have to be precise about these things. The appointments are fixed and precise down to the second, so I'm always very careful to do a count. It helps me keep things on schedule."

Leene's shoulders slumped as Death spoke.

Suddenly Death said, "Six . . ."

The number rang out like a shot. Instantly, Leene leaped back up. "This isn't right," he seethed. "I'm not ready to die. My company just tripled its profits. I've got things to do. You'll have to change your schedule."

Death shook his head. "What makes you think these things can be changed. Five . . ."

Leene leaped forward at the shadow trying to grab it. But it seemed to surround him.

"Who do you think you are?" he shouted. "If you really want to take me, then at least serve notice. Give me several days to think about it."

"It's not done that way," Death said patiently. "I come when I'm told, no sooner or later."

"Then who does? Tell me that. I'd like to speak to him."

Death sighed again. "You'll be appearing before Him soon enough," he said. "Four . . ."

"And who is He? God, I suppose?" Leene said sarcastically. "Well, I don't believe in Him."

"That doesn't matter," said Death. "Personal ideas about God don't change the fact of who or what He is."

For a moment, Leene was stunned. Somehow he'd always thought that one's belief or lack of it was the determining factor. He replied, "Well, He should have informed me about Himself."

Death's voice continued to intone with patience. "Do you have a Bible? Yes, I see it over on the shelf there. Aren't there churches in this neighborhood? Yes, I passed three on this very street. Hasn't your wife repeatedly expressed to you a desire that you repent and believe in Jesus? Of course. My records show, in fact, that various other relatives, several local pastors, two young people in your company, a man in your lodge, several people on the street, and numerous others have all mentioned to you about the need to believe and follow Christ. In each case, your conscience also reminded you to listen."

Leene sputtered and shook his head, but Death kept on. "In addition, our records show that over eight hundred thousand times—803,674 to be exact—throughout your 65 years on earth, you were reminded about wrong actions of every sort. In each case, it was recorded that according to principle your conscience told you that what you were doing was wrong both before, during, and after the acts of sin."

Leene clenched and unclenched his fist repeatedly on the handle of his pistol. "Tell me this, know-it-all, what about when I went forward for baptism in my church when I was twelve?"

Death wheezed a lengthy sigh. "The records show that this particular act was motivated by a desire to gain a certain medal in your Boy Scout troop."

"A lie!" shouted Leene. "You have no proof of that."

"Look," said Death. "I have a long night ahead of me. My responsibility is not to prove anything. Really, if you had considered that I would come some day you might have been better prepared."

Leene's mouth dropped. "Better prepared?! How did I know you were coming? You never sent me a note."

Death replied, "Every time you went to a funeral, every time you passed a graveyard, every time you had a brush with disaster I reminded you. In fact, as you have gone up in years, my reminders have come daily. Three . . ."

"But what about the millions who haven't heard?"

"First," said Death, "my Master always deals with everyone with perfect justice. So you can leave the matter of those who haven't heard to Him. Second, you have heard. You're responsible for you, not them."

Leene pointed the gun at the shadow. But he realized such a tactic was useless. Suddenly, an idea hit him. "Look, Death, I've heard of people being saved at the last minute, on their death beds. Is that possible?"

Death was quiet a moment. Then he said, "Yes, it's possible. I'm not usually one to say such things, but all things are possible with Him. I've seen many 'deathbed conversions,' as they're called. There's always time to repent and believe as long as you're alive."

"Then I could do it right now, right?"

"Of course. Any time so long as you're still alive. I would be very glad to see it." Death waited.

Leene screwed his face through several contortions, but somehow the more he thought about repenting the angrier he became. He found himself thinking, what right does God have to demand this of me? Why should I repent now? This is preposterous.

He turned again to Death. "Death, I need more time to think. I haven't had enough time. Come back tomorrow."

"I'm sorry," said Death. "As I understand it, He gives

each person precisely the time they need. If they don't do it by then, they never do it. So please allow me to do my duty. One . . ."

Leene fell to his knees. "Please, Death, I will repent. Just give me one more hour."

The shadow moved quickly and enveloped Leene. Leene fired the gun.

Death quietly said, "Zero," and as Leene slumped to the floor, Death glanced at Leene's watch and nodded.

Once again he had performed his service on the dot.

The next day the story took up a minute in the nightly news. It was mentioned that Leene had had a 300% year and also about the strange gunshot. But the investigators had come up with no clues as to whether an intruder had come into Leene's office. The anchorman even lit a cigar with a twenty dollar bill in Leene's honor. Turning to the weatherman, he remarked, "I guess when your number's up, it's up, isn't it, Bill?"

"Righto," said the weatherman, turning to the camera. "And your number may be up this weekend, folks, 'cause we've got a doosie for you."

Cute story.

But true.

Everyone will stand before You?

Everyone.

It makes me shudder.

There is no need for the believer to be afraid. When he stands before Me, there is no mention of sins, except to say that Jesus has paid for them.

Really?

Absolutely. Jesus' sacrifice is complete and perfect.

I'm glad I believe in Him.

That's good, but you must also follow Him.

I'm trying.

Do, don't just try. Now what else do you want to talk about?

Jesus

WHY DID YOU DO HIM THAT WAY?

In some ways, Father, Jesus is an enigma. God incarnate. Completely man, completely God. There seem like a lot of ways You might have come into our world, yet Jesus is the most . . .

Unexpected?

Somewhat.

Astonishing?

Definitely.

Perfect?

I wouldn't have thought of that.

What would you have thought of?

If I was God and I was to come into the world I'd created, to walk among people, be friends with men and women and children, speak words that transform, do deeds that validate my identity, I'd have done it in an age when television existed, when everyone could see everything, when everything could be easily proved.

You think that because He came at a time when the world was under Roman rule and when modern technology didn't exist His whole life and ministry are questionable?

Somewhat. I mean, today we could verify the miracles. We could have Him speak to the whole world instantly. We could record everything about Him. There would be no question of who He was.

What about all those who have gone before? The third century. The tenth century. The eighteenth century. Didn't they have a right to know Him?

Sure. But You could have had television and all of modern technology invented back then, couldn't You? Surely, You could have arranged for the whole thing to come off.

I couldn't just force inventions on the world. Certain scientific laws and principles have to be in place for modern technology to happen. Early history had to happen a certain way to lead to later history. Things don't happen in a vacuum. For the television to be invented, there first had to be the phonograph, the telephone, the radio, electricity, and the equipment to harness electricity. For those things to be in place, other inventions and ideas had to come to fore. I can create out of nothing, but man cannot invent out of nothing. All the forces, ideas, truths, and implements of previous times led to the forces, ideas, truths, and implements of later times. Even I will not simply drop an invention out of the sky for man to use and manipulate. Without the backdrop of everything else, it would be meaningless. A television in 32 A.D. wouldn't, first of all, have had a place to plug in.

A moot point.

Indeed. Everything requires a context. The television couldn't have been invented before the 20th century because the context wasn't there.

Okay, but why was Jesus born when He was? Were there reasons for Your choice?

Of course.

Can You name some?

The Roman peace, for one thing. Because of Roman rule, people in Jesus' age were able to move about fairly freely. Without the Roman peace, or Pax Romana, the Apostle Paul would not have evangelized much of the civilized world at the time.

Another factor was crucifixion. No other age had invented such a form of execution. If Jesus was to die, He had to die by some horrid means that all people would consider worthy of salvation, God, and redemption.

A third factor was Roman justice. Without its form of justice, Jesus would never have come to trial the way He did, He never would have been executed so unjustly and unrighteously. The Jews would not have had power over Him.

A fourth factor was the nature of eyewitness testimony. Today, scientists would want to perform experiments on Jesus' body, and when they couldn't, because He only appeared to His followers, and when He refused to yield to their methods, the whole hoax theory would be more critical. Imagine what Dan Rather would say when these Christians claim Christ is alive, but nobody but His followers can find Him? In effect, the resurrection is better proved by the eyewitness testimony and circumstances in which it happened than if it happened today. Those men and women died for their belief that Jesus was alive. Today, they'd be written off as nuts and weirdos, and their impact would be greatly diffused.

Those reasons make sense.

Consider the way the miracles happened. If Jesus lived today, the news media and other interest groups would all be clamoring for His attention and help. How could He possibly disciple the twelve? He needed an environment in which His public ministry could flourish and His private ministry achieve the results necessary. He had to nurture twelve men, one of whom was a traitor, so that they would turn the world upside down with their message. Today, Jesus would spend all His time in hospitals, emptying them. And what would happen when He refused to do the things the government or the media demanded? He'd be labeled an egotistical charlatan. In the first century, the environment allowed for Him to accomplish His mission of redemption, discipleship, and legacy without compromising His divinity. That could never happen today.

And what of building relationships? Today, Jesus would be a celebrity, not a Messiah. He'd have no time for real people, the very people He needed to influence and transform. In the cocoon of first century Israel, He had the best time and place to develop the kind of relationships that would lead to eternal succor and salvation.

For these reasons and many more, the first century was the perfect time for Jesus to come, the fullness of time, as the Apostle Paul put it.

I guess I buy that.

You'd better. It's the only thing I'm selling.

Hmmmm.

Why Did Jesus Die?

Many of the things You've told me make a lot of sense. However, I still don't understand why Jesus had to die. Wasn't there any other way?

There are two issues involved. Man's sin and My character. My holiness demands that sin be banished, extinguished, eliminated completely from My sphere of influence. My righteousness demands that right be done in all cases, that I must deal with everyone in a righteous manner. My justice calls for justice being carried out. For every crime, there is a penalty. For every penalty, there is a punishment. These three elements of My character conspire against mankind because they have committed abominable crimes. Not all of them. But all have sinned. None has lived a perfect life in thought, word, or deed except one, Jesus. My holiness, righteousness, and justice all clamor that someone pay for what these people have done and that their sins be dealt with promptly, completely, and finally. That's an awesome task.

But why couldn't You just forgive us?

Under certain conditions I could. But these three qualities forbid forgiveness. Furthermore, forgiveness doesn't deal with the real problem. The problem of sin remains. All forgiveness does is wipe out the penalty for sin in specific cases. What of future sin? What of sin in heaven? If all I did was forgive, heaven would be planet earth all over again. No, sin has to be dealt with in a final, surpassing, all-encompassing, and just sense.

Couldn't You just declare amnesty?

Same thing as forgiveness. It doesn't work when I have to deal with Myself internally. Forgiveness overlooks My holiness, My righteousness, My justice. What of all those people who were unfairly imprisoned, wounded, punished, or killed in this life? Do they not deserve justice? What of all those who would enter heaven without changing an iota of their attitudes and hatreds? Can you imagine Hitler in heaven? Stalin? Attila? Caesar? No, these people would immediately begin wreaking havoc all over the universe if I simply declared amnesty and let them participate in the new creation.

Then what is the answer?

There are three other qualities that balance the three I've just told you about. My love, which wants to embrace and nurture My people. My mercy, which hungers to forgive and forget. And My grace, which wants to offer heaven, eternal life, and all the good gifts of the inheritance to all My creatures. Do you see the dilemma?

No.

If I forgive and forgo the penalty of sin, I compromise My righteousness, holiness, and justice. If I punish and consign sinful people to hell, I compromise My love, My mercy, and My grace.

There has to be answer.

There is. In Jesus. When Jesus went to the cross, He paid the penalty for sin, satisfying My holiness, righteousness, and justice. At the same time, He released My grace, love, and mercy to be given to all who would trust Him.

So Jesus had to die?

He had to agree to die in eternity past before I ever even created the world, or I would have had to destroy the world the moment sin entered it.

So Jesus really did take our sins onto Himself when He died on that cross?

Absolutely. And His death and sacrifice are available to anyone who believes. It's that simple.

So all we have to do is cast ourselves on Christ, figuratively speaking.

No, in reality. You truly do cast yourself on Jesus. You truly do rely and trust and depend on Him for everything. It's the key to the whole process. Through the trust in Him and the confession of sin and repentance that follows, one is cleansed, one is forgiven, one is inhabited by the Spirit, and the process of transformation begins.

So we are made fit for heaven?

Precisely. Without the act of trust, and the active quality of trust in Him, a person does not undergo fundamental change internally. He is the same as he always was. The thrust of the Gospel is not only that you'll be forgiven and receive eternal life, but that you'll be transformed, that the Spirit will work in your life and change you gradually into the likeness of Jesus. This process goes on until death, at which time perfection is attained. But only for those who believe. For those who do not believe, it's as if Christ has done nothing for them. They're on their own and must face the consequences of standing before Me as the just, righteous and holy Creator.

Dangerous ground.

Indeed. I would not wish it on anyone.

Without Christ, we are truly lost.

Absolutely, with no hope of anything but absolute justice carried out to its absolute extreme. As one of your own writers has said, "There are those who say to God, 'Thy will be done,' and those to whom God says, 'Thy will be done.'" No one in his right mind should want to stand before Me naked, bearing his sins with him. Everyone of those sins will receive an exact punishment.

So hell is the just recompense of an unbelieving soul?

Yes.

You speak some hard words.

We are not playing games here. The act of redemption was the most costly and dear act in the universe. Nothing else even comes close in the cost.

What was the cost?

Eternal separation from Me.

Jesus was separated from You for eternity?

When Jesus languished on that cross, He felt the impact of an eternity separated from His Father. It is the only time in our relationship that we have not been one. It cost us dearly. But we believed the joy of saving mankind was the honorable result, and we were willing to pay it.

You and Jesus are no longer separated?

No.

But if He was separated for eternity from You, how can He now be one with You?

I said He experienced the force and power of eternal punishment and separation. No man could have endured it for even a microsecond. But because He was God, the second person of the trinity, He could. And He did.

Amazing grace.

Yes, it is amazing. To some degree, I'm amazed we did it. We could have chosen not to create anything, or to create creatures who were not free. But that was not our goal and purpose. Free creatures in Our image, able to love and give and sacrifice voluntarily and live in holiness for all eternity, are a worthy price, though not an equal one.

Equal?

The price Jesus paid in terms of agony, pain, and punishment was far higher than if all mankind was thrown into hell and made to pay for their sins forever.

That seems impossible.

With man it is impossible but not with God.

You're always blowing me away.

That is not My intent, but I'm glad you're a bit awed. It's the whole reason the church exists, that I inspire worship. If We had not done anything for mankind, We would still be worthy of your worship and love. But it would not seem as magnificent. Jesus is the true hero, perhaps the only true hero. Hollywood has painted some astonishing pictures of heroes and heroines, but most of them are fictional. Real heroes are hard to find. A man who will risk his life for someone else, a stranger, an orphan, is a rarity, but he should be applauded. A man who will die in the place of someone about to be shot by the Nazis, especially if the one died for is a good, honest man, is a blessing. It was done. A priest died for others in the camps. We love him for it. But who would die for criminals? Who would die a horrid, excruciating death for criminals? Who would die a horrid, excruciating death for criminals who disdained the person dying in their place? And who would die a horrid, excruciating death for criminals who disdained the person dying and do it at pain of eternal torment and the utter and unequivocal rejection of God? That is a death to be revered, to be praised, to be accepted as a gift of the most towering proportions. That is the death Jesus died.

Amazing. But why?

Because He loved you. Loved you, before you were ever born, before you had ever shown any potential or gift, before you had done anything good or bad. He did it for you willingly and gladly. If you were the only one lost, He would have done it for you alone. His love is so great that He could not have done anything else.

When He was in the Garden that last night, when He prayed that He would not have to go to the cross, could He have walked away?

Absolutely. It was His decision. I would not force Him. That would have gone against every holy organ in My spirit.

But He chose to go?

Yes.

Because He loved me?

Never leave the "me" out, friend. Dying for the sins of the whole world is an intangible thing. Dying for "me" is right up front, right in My face. Let Me make it a bit more real.

Imagine this Frenchman who loves a woman in Canada. He wants to marry her. He's extremely powerful and wealthy. He has vast holdings all over the world, an intelligence network, and knows everything about her. Her name is Katy, she's a servant girl and her master is a cruel, snarl-lipped cur. He has no intention of letting her go and uses her for whatever purposes he designs.

The Frenchman begins to act. He starts by writing her a letter. When Katy reads it, she thinks, "Some prank, no doubt. Who'd be interested in me, a scrubwoman?"

The Frenchman doesn't give up. In his second letter, he speaks of his own life and situation, mentions some of his favorite activities, reveals plans he has for the future.

After that, it's gifts. They arrive in big packages, left at the door. Her master even brings them by. "Looks like you've got a friend somewhere. Well, wait till he sees your face. Then we'll see how much he wants you. Ha."

It's true. Katy's face is not pretty. She is slightly deformed. A hairlip. A terrible scar from her master. A hump. She writes back to the Frenchman. "Why are you doing this? I can offer you nothing."

A telegram comes the next day. "I do not seek what you can offer, I seek you."

That afternoon Katy hurries off to the woods to gather

sticks for her master's fire. As she bends to pick up the kindling, a grizzly bear lumbers toward her. Katy turns to run. Then, just as suddenly, a man appears, lifts a rifle, and fires a warning shot. The grizzly turns and runs. Katy asks who the man is. "I was sent by the Frenchman," he says and disappears.

A week later her master storms into the house. "You've run up a bill at the grocer's. I never told you to buy all that food. Now you must pay."

The grocer threatens prison. But at the last moment messengers from the Frenchman bring checks. "We will pay for everything."

After that, the Frenchman sends his friends to talk to her. They answer her questions, provide insights about him, and express to her the Frenchman's own words of love and kindness. Katy remains unsure. No proposal has yet been offered, and besides this Frenchman might turn out to be a very ugly little man, though nice on the inside.

So the Frenchman sends his photo album with pictures of his exploits. He describes his adventures in detail, shows her evidence of his true powers.

Katy is amazed. He isn't an ugly little man after all. Yet, somehow she isn't ready for a commitment. She knows she is not pretty. She knows how people stare at her. Why me? she wonders. Why now? What does he really want?

Bad as her master is, he does feed her and keep her clothed and under a roof.

Finally, the Frenchman himself appears. He's all she could have hoped for and more. Handsome, courteous, gentle. She's nearly in love. But one thing nags at her: What if he changes his mind, now that he's seen me? Or what if when I'm old he decides he likes another? How can I know he really loves me?

When she goes home that night she pulls out the old pictures of her master and looks longingly at him. He isn't so bad. Could she really give him up for this Frenchman?

All these things are swirling about in her head when the police whirl up with shouts and weapons. They inform her she is under arrest. Charges have been pressed (by the master), and she has to go to court.

They go to court and a long list of crimes is read off. The girl is broken and frightened, for it's all true. The judge rules that she'll be shot at dawn.

She is in despair. She had such high hopes. But how she is to die. What good is the Frenchman or any marriage they might have had? She weeps in her cell and hates her life, her master, her God, and the Frenchman, too.

The next morning the Frenchman comes to her cell, tells her he loves her, and that she's not going to die. He has a plan. She's amazed, but she doesn't see how he can help. He assures her it's all taken care of. She is to go free. That afternoon, she is released. But she pauses at the gate and watches the inner courtyard. What is to happen? What has the Frenchman done?

Suddenly, the police appear with the Frenchman. They march him out to the firing squad and tie him up. At the last moment, the Frenchman looks in her direction and smiles, and then the guns roar. Katy runs away, crazed with despair and pain. She knows now what the Frenchman has done, and she craves only to tell him thanks, to see him, to feel his touch again. She goes to her room, sits down, and weeps. She sees now how great his love was. And he's gone.

Three days pass. Then, without warning, the Frenchman is standing before her, alive and handsome as always. He takes her in his arms and explains to her that he has the power to rise from the dead. Now he wants to know, "Will you marry me?"

She steps back. "But look at me," she says, "I'm crippled. I'm ugly. I'm deformed. Why? What have I done for you?"

"Nothing," the Frenchman says. "I love you as you are."

"Then what is it that you see I will do for you?" she wails. "There must be something?"

The Frenchman smiles. "I love you as you are, Katy, not what you will do for me, ever. Just accept My love, please, and all things will be made right."

She stands there, amazed, and in love. There can be no question of her answer. She nods and they embrace. Instantly, she finds she is transformed. Her ugliness is gone. Her deformity removed. The scar is replaced by a beautiful dimple. She is altogether lovely. As she looks at herself, she cries, "But what has happened?"

"Love has transformed you," he says. Then he gives her a kiss, and sits her down. "I must go prepare our future home," he says, "but soon I will come back. We'll be married in a wonderful ceremony. Will you wait for me?"

She answers, "I will wait forever, because I know now you love me. Do what you have to do. I will wait until you return."

The story of redemption and Jesus.

Yes.

What can I say but thank You, thank You with all of my soul?

That is all I ask. And follow My Son.

That is easy after all You've done for me.

Predestination

Father, predestination really troubles me.

It troubles most of you.

Why?

You probably feel it leaves you without any control. Everything happens at My command and whim. Most people don't like that idea.

The way You just said it, for instance.

I said it like people think it is. In reality, predestination is a precious truth that guarantees your salvation. It ultimately means that I have planned out—predestined—certain events to happen that will insure you have the opportunity to believe and be redeemed.

It doesn't negate my free will?

Not at all. It works with your will and insures that you will be ready at the proper time.

That doesn't sound like I've heard it taught.

I've heard it taught many ways that aren't true. But once again, let Me give you a story that illustrates it. Maybe that will settle your mind.

I'm here.

I'd like to tell the story from the point of view of a lost person.

Go ahead.

I couldn't remember quite how I got into the river, though I felt it was pleasant. The river rolled along, pitching us here and there, eddying and playing, spraying our faces. We had plenty of time for talk and cards and whatnot. No one had any particularly enchanting explanation for how it all started. Of course, there were speculations.

Some said we'd been here all along; it never ended; the river just went on and on.

Others said we were a part of it; we'd grown up and changed with it.

Still others remarked that there was no need to question, just to enjoy.

And then there were those who said it wasn't always like this, but some ancestral sin had put us into it.

Just the same, it didn't seem so bad, if you were one of the rich ones, or had everything taken care of.

Then the rescuer arrived. He was this burly, friendly fellow. He didn't talk much. But suddenly he was there in the river next to me. I had been sipping some River-ade while watching one of our troupes put on a water polo exhibition. When I turned my head, he was there.

"I've come to rescue you," he said. He began to put his arm over my chest.

"Wait," I cried. "Rescue me from what? I didn't know I needed rescuing."

He said quietly, "The river is running towards a waterfall. You'll be dashed on the rocks."

I laughed. "I've heard about the waterfall. Many say it's not true."

"It's true," he said.

Something about the way he said things rang fear through my bones. But I countered, "How do I know it's true?"

"It's true," he said. "There is no need of proof except that I say it's true."

I snickered. "And who are you to go about telling everyone you know the truth?"

"I'm the rescuer," he said. "Whatever I say is, by its very nature, true. I can't speak anything but truth. You can rely on me for that. And you, I assure you, are headed for the waterfall."

"What if I don't go along with this?" I asked. "What if I refuse?"

He replied, "That's your choice. I will take whatever action I choose in such an event."

It was a startling answer. Nothing threw him. He stayed calm.

"Where will you take me?" I asked.

"To safety."

"Where is that?"

"I'll show you."

I laughed again. "You speak in circles. This doesn't make any sense."

"It will," he said.

I shook my head, smiling. "You're the strangest person I've ever met."

This time he chuckled. "Many say that. But I've come to rescue you. Are you ready?"

I gulped. "You're being rather pushy about this."

He said, "I won't force you. Would you rather I left you alone?"

"But what if I decided I wanted rescue later?"

"I might not be available later."

I gulped again. I searched his eyes to see if this wasn't some new lie. I'd seen a lot of lies in the river. You learned to trust no one, not even yourself. But I could detect no falsehood.

"Okay," I said. "Take me."

He put his arm over my chest and began pulling me toward the bank of the river. I'd seen it often enough before. A desolate place. No one but fools went there. No one quite understood how they got there. But everyone was sure there was no reason to go there. It was cold and damp and appeared lifeless.

The rescuer set me upon the shore. "Make yourself at home and move inland. Whenever you want to talk, call me. I'll come, and we'll talk. If you need anything, just ask. Only keep moving inland. Also, think of any you know in the river that you want me to rescue. I'll be asking you frequently for names."

He paused. Then he said with grave precision, "Whatever you do, don't go back into the river, no matter who tells you. I don't make it a habit to pull out people twice."

I swallowed and watched as he dove back into the river. Already he was speaking with another.

I noticed the ground was hard. The air was cold. I saw others wandering around on the bank. Some appeared lost. One, I noticed, dove back into the river. But several were making their way inland.

I turned back to the river, and suddenly I was struck with the most incredible longing.

"Just a quick dive," said a voice. "You'll be warm again."

But I remembered the rescuer's words and hesitated.

The voice said again, "How do you know he's right? A quick dive can't hurt."

"But he said," I protested, "I shouldn't do it."

"But why?" said the voice. "What harm can there be?"

I thought about it. "Because he said so," I said. Something within me had changed. I liked the solid feel of the ground. Not a whole lot. It hurt my feet. But it gave one a contented feeling. Not like the river—always changing; never knowing what was coming next.

I began watching the rescuer. He was pulling people out all over the river. He worked quickly. Twice I saw him strike a man in the jaw and knock him out to get him out of the river. On another occasion, I watched him argue for nearly an hour. That man also succumbed. But then there were others. There were some he approached and after only a brief conversation, he left them. I never saw him rescue them. There was one he argued with for several hours, then stopped abruptly. He left him swirling along alone. Two of them, I observed, he talked to several times, went and rescued others inbetween, then came back to them. One he finally did rescue. The other, I don't know.

The amazing thing was that everyone was approached by him at least once, and many were approached often. I couldn't see how he could keep it up, but he did.

As he rescued more and more people, a small group was gathering around me. We began to talk.

"Isn't it wonderful," said one. "He rescued all of us from the waterfall."

"Yeah, but how do we know there's really a waterfall?" asked another.

No one had an answer. But someone said, "I guess we just have to trust him."

Most agreed. But one was angry. "I think it's wrong that he barges into my quiet existence and demands to rescue me. I'm going back into the river."

Several tried to stop the man. But he dove in. We didn't

see him again.

We began walking inland together. But one turned back and watched the rescuer for awhile. When he caught up to us, he was angry. "He didn't rescue my Uncle Pete."

Soon the whole group was in a state of upset.

"Yeah, and my father went down towards the waterfall too," another said. "The rescuer only talked to him once that I saw."

A third remembered a sister who wasn't rescued. It seemed everyone had someone he didn't rescue.

"He's a bit unfair about this," said one, "rescuing some and letting others go."

I replied, "But he approached them all."

"He could've knocked them out," answered another.

"That's what he did to me. I'm glad that he did that to me. But why didn't he do that in other cases if they wouldn't go along with him?"

We had no answers.

"Perhaps we ought to ask him. That's what he told me to do," I said.

"Right," answered another. "Let's ask him."

We all began shouting out our request and instantly the rescuer was among us. Each brought out his protest. "Why didn't you rescue my mother?" "What about my sister, Jo?" "How come you didn't knock out my cousin Anthony?" And, "Why did you only talk once to my card partner, Bill?"

The rescuer was silent a long time. We all waited, somewhat impatiently. Finally, he said, "I choose to rescue whom I will rescue. I choose when to start and complete a rescue, and when to leave it off. That is my choice; I'm the rescuer."

"But what did they do," cried another, "to make you

leave off?"

"Many things," said the rescuer. "Some argued, some fought, some dove back in. There are many reasons I choose not to rescue a person."

"Then what did we do that made you rescue us?" asked still another.

The rescuer smiled. "Nothing."

Instantly, the group exploded with anger. "Nothing!" shouted one. "You rescued us for no reason?"

"Not 'no reason,'" said the rescuer. "I rescued you for reasons known only to myself. But, I assure you, it had nothing to do with anything about you, or in you, or that you did. I chose to rescue you because I loved you."

Everyone was silent for sometime after this.

But then a lady voiced the question that was on all our hearts. "But why did you love us? There must be some reason."

"Because I'm love itself," said the rescuer.

"You mean there was nothing in us or about us that made you love us?" said the woman, miffed and unhappy.

"Nothing," said the rescuer quietly.

We were all very frightened and worried about this.

But the rescuer went on. "Think of it this way. My love and choice of you is not dependent on anything about you or in you. It's totally dependent on me. That should give you great security."

Frankly, I didn't know what to think. But it did make sense. In fact, the more I thought about it, the more settled I felt. Finally, I said, "If this is so, then we have every reason to love you all the more."

The rescuer said nothing.

Suddenly, another member of the group said, "But why

don't you rescue all of them?"

The rescuer was quiet again. Then he said, "That is not how I've chosen to do it."

"But why?" said another. "Why don't you choose to do it another way?"

The rescuer peered into our faces. He said, "Don't you do as you please with what is yours? I do as I please with what is mine."

I said, "You mean you own us, the river, everything?"

"Yes."

Now everyone was upset. But then a small voice, a child, spoke from the back of the group. "Why did you rescue me?"

Everyone turned and looked at the little boy. He was deformed, ugly. He couldn't even walk upright. No one had noticed him before.

The rescuer's eyes were tender. "Because I love you."

"As much as everyone else?" said the lad, a tear forming in his eye. It was obvious he'd known much pain in the river.

"I love everyone equally," said the rescuer, "but I also love them infinitely. I love you infinitely also. There is no end of my love for you."

Some members of the group were weeping now.

My own throat was feeling a little taut, but I managed to say, "What if you hadn't rescued us?"

"You would go over the waterfall and be killed."

"But isn't there some other way?" another replied.

"None," he said. He didn't say this like it was an unhappy state of affairs, or that he wished it was otherwise. He just said it.

"But if you didn't rescue us, wouldn't someone else?"

"There is no one else," he said.

I gulped. "But if there's nothing about us that makes us

worthy, the amazing thing is that you rescue anyone."

The rescuer gazed steadily at us, saying nothing.

"But how did we get into the river?" said someone in the back with a beard. "It seems that the whole problem is being in the river."

The rescuer looked him firmly in the eye. "You put yourself in the river," he said.

We all gasped. I'd heard it before, but I never really believed it.

The man seemed bent on pressing this, though. He said, "When? I don't remember that."

"After the beginning."

"You mean we weren't always in the river?"

"No."

He let this sink in, and seemed about to turn to go, but a large man jumped up and gestured a moment. "Can I say something?" he asked.

"Begin," said the rescuer.

"It seems to me that if we put ourselves into the river, couldn't get out on our own, and would have gone over the waterfall if you didn't do something, then you have done us a great service."

Everyone agreed.

"Then," said the man, "although I don't have much, I want to offer you my life for service and worship. Will you accept it?"

The rescuer gazed steadily at all of us. It seemed as he caught my eye, that he looked right through me, right into the very depths of my soul. I quivered and suddenly felt very afraid in his presence. Then, almost without thinking, I knelt before him and said, "You are my lord. I will follow you wherever you go."

I can't quite explain it, but that moment was astounding. He didn't act as though we had done him a great service, nor did he appear to think of our deeds as nothing. It was as though he recognized this was as it should be. He enjoyed it, and yet at the same time he desired it without demanding it.

Then, just as suddenly, he cried, "To the uplands! Move inward and upward. Run! You must learn more."

We all began to move. Some ran, some walked, some labored, limping and tired. But all of us moved onward, helping one another, encouraging one another.

Few, if any, ever looked back again to the river with longing.

That explains a lot about predestination and all those other heavy doctrines that theologians talk about.

It is a simple answer.

I like it.

The question is, what will you do with it?

I will follow You and offer my life in service to You forever.

Then you will do well.

Satan

THE NEVERENDING BATTLE

Let's talk about Satan, Father.

I'm here.

Well, explain to me what happened. How did Satan come to be Your greatest and most cunning adversary?

I created him as the height of my powers. He had every gift, every mark of beauty, every perfection. He was the leading cherub of heaven, the covering cherub, the one who protected My holiness. Over time, he led the orchestras of heaven in the most beatific music you can imagine. He was a brilliant conductor and worship leader. But he became proud and jealous.

Jealous?

He wanted to be worshiped. He saw that We alone were worshiped and exalted in heaven, even though all possessed a place of privilege, power and exultation. He wanted what we had. In time, he marshalled a third of heaven against me, promising them position, honor, and glory in his king-dom. Unfortunately, they believed him. I warned them over and over of the danger of their thinking. They would not listen. Soon, a rebellion occurred. Heaven and earth were laid desolate. The universe was plunged into turmoil and destruction. Angels warred against angels. And Lucifer, the name I had given Satan before he became Satan, warred against Me. He tried to destroy Me, but I am God and cannot be destroyed. He greatly overestimated his powers, and greatly underestimated mine. He was thrust out of heaven with his rebels and heaven was restored.

Where does earth come in?

I had a third of heaven arrayed against Me. Many of the remaining angels were skeptical, doubtful, and wanted to know why they should remain loyal to Me. Satan told them I was not worthy of their love or respect, so I chose to conduct an incredible experiment in which they could observe and learn of My character, all the while having the opportunity to serve and know Me in heaven. I created earth as a place where I would show all of My attributes. The angels would record their observations and thoughts, and at the end of human history, there would be a judgment to see how everything came out. Was I worthy of their respect and loyalty, or was Satan? At the same time, I would bring about the redemption of mankind and the enthronement in heaven of My people who were created in My image. Though mankind is lower than the angels in intellect and power, it is higher in the hierarchy of Creation. I have chosen to make them the rulers and the angels the servants.

Interesting juxtaposition. Can Satan win this war?

No. He has already lost.

When?

At the cross and resurrection. There Jesus destroyed Satan's singular power, that of death, and eliminated his one advantage—the judgment of sin. He is beaten and done for.

Does he know that?

He doesn't believe it, though he knows it in his deepest heart. Meanwhile, he wages his losing war, thinking somehow it will turn out differently.

That makes no sense.

Not to Me. But to him, it does. What choice does he have? Perhaps I can tell you a story to illustrate how it works.

I'm all ears.

Natas and the King sat down to the chessboard. They had had many such games. Every match was a master lesson in intrigue and trickery from Natas, and flawless, sacrificial, but wise action on the King's part.

The King always won. Sometimes a match went on through many games with the King down one, two, or three games. But in the end, he had a way of always turning it around, even the apparently bad moves for good. No one quite understood it.

But, of course, not once had the King lost his most important piece, the queen. And it was said that Natas had learned a strategy that would take it.

The two players sat at the board: Natas, slit-eyed and crafty; the King, his palm open and plaintive.

Then Natas spoke words no one expected or knew. "We

play to the death," he said. "One final game."

Natas had won many single games. It was the length of a match that always wore him down, that gave the King a chance to use his masterful wisdom. But one game? Just one? How could the King agree?

Natas was a shriveled, ugly man, once the handsomest in the realm. But his constant intrigue, shrewd plots, and harrowing escapes had turned him into a brown, wrinkled prune. Sour and sharp-tongued, he rarely lost a duel.

Until now. This would be his mightiest eclipse.

Or his final collapse.

"If that is what you desire," said the King.

The host inside the throneroom recoiled with shock at Natas's challenge, but anyone who had long observed the growing conflict knew it was coming to this.

"You are certain you want this?" asked the King. He seemed confident, yet anyone could tell he did not welcome the contest.

"Absolutely!" said Natas.

The King sighed. "All right, when do we begin?" Always calm, always sure. But perhaps too sure, this time. Natas was a shrewd one. Mighty in word and thought. Crafty in plot. He was known to topple whole legions with a single sly piece of trickery.

"Today," said Natas, with a curl of his lip. "Today! And it will go to the end. To the death."

"You know the rules?" The King held up the Book. It's black cover glistened in the radiant light of the King's breastplate.

"I know your rules," Natas the prime minister said contemptuously.

The rules. That was the means by which the King usually outfoxed the fox. Always there was something within them that was so clear, so transparent, Natas had missed it in his feverish determination to overthrow the King. No one violated them or could violate them. Even though Natas had tried many a time with lesser opponents, an appeal to the rules was enough to stop him from intrigue.

But Natas also had a reputation. The feint. The fake. The sly trick. Many had tromped unknowing into his traps, and fallen.

The King put the Book down on the table. "Then we will begin."

The board was set. King, Queen, Rook, Bishop, Knight, Pawn. Arranged as we all know it. The master game of games. The duel of nerves and mind.

The host drew near and watched as the King sat at the table, taking the white. Natas always took black. "I like to see him make the first mistake—at the very start," he said. "The rest is easy."

The King lined up his players. Natas followed. Then it was the King's move. He made the standard first step. The King's pawn two spaces forward. Nothing dramatic.

Natas did the same.

Already a hush had fallen on the host. Already bets were being made. But how could anyone bet against the King?

Easily. Natas already had a third of the host on his side. Perhaps as the game moved along, more would retreat or even desert one side for another. This was unto death. The great sword hung on the wall above the Game Table.

The King moved again—king's knight to king's bishop two.

Nothing remarkable.

Natas made a similar move, but it was the queen's knight

this time, to queen's bishop two.

The game was on.

It went back and forth. Natas claimed a pawn. The King took one also.

Natas took a bishop. The king took a knight.

Then, Natas laid a trap. It was a simple one. Every one of the host saw it immediately. The King wouldn't trip on that one. It was too simple. A bishop, knight, queen combination. Three blows, and the King would lose a rook.

And then the King moved—right into the trap. There was no escape.

A cry went up in the gallery. More bets were flying. But the faithful stood aghast and terrified. They knew well what Natas would do with them, given the chance.

Natas smiled and rubbed his hands together. He snatched the rook from the board as he laid his queen in its place. As he did, he kissed it and threw it into the air, then whipped out his sword and flailed it over his head.

The rook shattered.

"We don't play again, so why not destroy the pieces as they fall!" he shouted.

The King merely shook his head and made his next move. But he was down a rook now. It was an important heist. How could it have been that simple?

Still, the King remained calm. He moved deftly, certainly. The play went on with little action. Feints. Attempts at traps. Escapes and defensive measures.

Then the host watched in horror. No trap was laid. But the King appeared to be setting himself up. In another move he would lose his second bishop and a knight.

And claim nothing from Natas.

Was he laying a complex trap, too deep for mortal minds

to comprehend?

Needless to say, Natas sprang. His glee was almost palpable. He jumped, shouting, "There is no trick! The King has become senile!"

He took the bishop and knight in two swift moves.

What was the King doing? Didn't he understand this was unto death? He seemed to be stuck in a pattern. Nothing less than far superior wisdom could win now. Even a youngster could win against these odds.

But the King was king. He was wise. There had to be something else? But what?

Everyone knew it would have something to do with the rules, rules that Natas knew well, but years of intrigue and deception kept him from seeing their real power and truth.

Then Natas stooped to make more moves. He sacrificed a bishop, a pawn.

Then: he had the King cornered again. The King's forces appeared too weak to withstand the assault. And this time he took the King's second rook and two pawns.

The host strained to see a bead of sweat, a sign of fear on the King's face. But he was impassive. Was he not afraid of losing all—his kingdom, his life?

The King moved calmly, quietly, without a word. They exchanged pawns.

Now the King was left with one knight, the queen, and several pawns.

Natas still had both rooks, one bishop, his queen, and one more pawn than the King. The host sat so quiet, you could hear the King's breathing. It remained calm, sure. How could he be so?

Then suddenly the King's queen appeared entrapped. How could it have happened so fast? The queen! Never before had he lost a queen. Never. If he lost the queen, all hope was gone. Natas would triumph. That was beyond certainty. That was carved in stone high as a mountain.

As Natas closed in, it seemed all breathing stopped.

And then he had her. The King's queen. Even at the expense of a rook and the bishop, it was nothing. Nothing!

The moment the rook took the square where the queen stood, Natas leaped up, snatching the queen away in his hand. He held it to his lips and kissed the little figurine. "The queen! I have won the queen! I have won! I have won!" He held it up for all to see. Then in his wretched, clawlike hands, he crushed the queen to bits of stone. What was left, he put under his heel and rubbed it deep into the carpet.

Then he eyed the King. "Do you resign now?" Already he reached to grab the sword on the wall.

But the King shook his head. "The game is not yet over. Play on." He had a knight, his king, and three pawns. Natas still possessed a rook and his queen, as well as other minor pieces.

The room was dead quiet. The whole host fixed their eyes on the face of the King. He reached to the board and made a movement. A pawn. Forward.

"A useless move!" cried Natas with a laugh. "It will never make the other side of the board!"

Natas ignored the pawn, still several moves from the other side, and bored in on the King's king with his rook. He would have him in less than four moves.

The King moved the pawn again.

Natas set up his queen. His bishop would be next.

The King moved the king back one space.

Natas would be set up in one more move. Checkmate. And then: death!

The King put his hand over the board. Every eye fixed on his fingers. What had he picked up? Not the pawn. Not the knight, or the king. What had been there?

The gallery strained to see. Then he moved his piece. It would certainly be his last move.

But his hand concealed the piece. He set it down and held it in place—blocking Natas' final descent. What was the piece? What could it have been? The King had no piece that could be moved there.

Then the King took his hand away.

The queen! The same queen Natas had crushed into the rug. How? Where? And it had cornered one of Natas' rooks, eliminating the possible checkmate.

The host gasped.

Natas roared. "What is this?"

The King said nothing.

Natas jumped up. "This is a cheat. There is no second queen. I have already destroyed the only one there was. And your pawn has not reached the other side of the board!"

The King picked up the Book with the black cover. "I asked you if you had read the rules before we began."

Natas ripped the Book out of the King's hand. "I have read the rules. What mischief is this?"

The King calmly took the Book from Natas and pointed to a passage. Natas read. Then his face flared crimson as blood. "Unjust!" he shrieked. "Unfair! The King's queen cannot be restored after three moves never to be taken again! Impossible!"

"Those are the rules," the King said quietly.

"But it's not fair! How can anyone play such a game?" screamed Natas, his hair standing out on his neck, his lips blue, his eyes red and full of fire.

"You know the rules. Play on," said the King.

Natas sputtered, turned to the gallery, screamed obscenities. "This is not fair. I refuse."

The King stood up. "You're the one who posed the challenge. But if you want to desist, we will stop. All you must do then is bow to me."

"Never!" screamed Natas. He looked at the board and was about to move.

But then he pushed himself back from the table. "If the King's queen can never be taken again," he said, banging his fist on the table, "then I can never win!"

The King set his jaw. "And who suggested you ever should or could win?"

Natas' eyes popped and saliva drooled off his lip. "That's the way it is with games!" he screamed. "Everyone learns that in Kindergarten. Each side has a fair chance at winning."

The King set his jaw and shook his head. "This isn't a game," he said quietly. "It is not played like a game. Not the way you have chosen to play it."

Natas leaned forward, his hands white on the edges of the playing table. "Then I can never win this contest. Never! Is that correct?"

"That is correct," said the King curtly.

Natas pulled his hair and looked to the gallery for help. But no one said a word.

"Then why should I even play?" he screamed. "Why should I even challenge you if I can never win?"

The King gazed evenly at Natas for a moment. Then he walked to the board and took Natas' rook with his untakable queen. "Your move!" he said quietly.

Natas knocked over the players on the board and came around the table, whipping out his sword. "Answer me," he shrieked. "Why should I even play if I can't win?"

The King pushed the sword away from his chest. "You must answer that one yourself, Natas. It is something I will never comprehend."

Suddenly, Natas lifted his hand and swiped across the King's neck with his sword.

The sword shattered the moment it touched the King. The King turned to his guards. They grabbed and held Natas.

"Then what am I supposed to do," he screamed, "if I can never win?"

"Lay down your arms," said the King quietly. "Cease the rebellion. Change your mind. Give it up and come back and do what you were chosen to do."

Natas seemed to be thinking, grasping at anything that might help him in that moment. "But what if I can win?"

"You can't."

Natas seethed, "How do I know you're telling me the truth?"

The King sighed and shook his head, pointing his finger at Natas. "You have to choose whether you believe I am or not. But I am telling you the truth. You can never win, and if you continue in this, you will end up locked in the deepest dungeon of my kingdom where you will no longer have opportunity to influence and hurt others."

Natas shrieked then, a horrid, obscene shriek. "Then I'll kill you!" he screamed. "I'll kill you!"

The King was calm. "I repeat: you cannot do that. You will never do that."

Natas struggled, but the guards held him.

"Take him out," the King said calmly. "And all who are with him."

A huge entourage was taken out screaming and kicking.

But when they were outside the palace, they stood on the edge hurling insults at the King who stood on the wall.

Suddenly, Natas stood up high and strong among them, having now freed himself from the guards. "We'll take you!" he shouted. "We'll find a way."

"There is no way," the King said quietly and turned away.

"Don't turn your back to me, Scoundrel!" shouted Natas.

The King went back to the throneroom where the chess board sat. The din outside gradually subsided. Soon it was reported that Natas had gone into the forest, presumably to make plans to attack.

"What will we do?" asked the King's general.

The King bowed his head and sighed. Slowly, he picked up the pieces on the table. "Contain him," said the King. "We will not allow him to do further harm than is necessary."

"Will he ever turn back?" asked the general.

"No," said the King. "His pride has taken too deep a root."

"Then why let him live?"

The King sighed. "For now it is necessary."

"But why?" The pain in the general's voice was evident.

The King fixed him with his eyes. "To insure that you yourself and the others will not also rebel."

The general appeared even more pained. "I will never rebel, your Majesty."

"I know," said the King with a slight smile. He gently touched the general's shoulder with his hand. "Now I would like to be alone."

The general turned toward the door and signalled to the others to leave.

Then the King sat down and held the queen chess piece. For a long time he gripped it in his palm. Then when everyone was gone, the King closed his eyes and quietly wept.

So Satan really can never win?

That is correct.

It's a pity. Such a waste.

All evil is a waste.

I'm beginning to understand that.

Good. Then we are getting somewhere.

Always.

Two Stories Of Destiny

I will tell you two final stories that I'd just like to leave as is. And then we shall move on. Agreed?

Agreed.

I hope you will be moved.

One Destiny

Consciousness slowly broke through the haze in Jeremiah Delms' mind. He had been sitting in church. Every Sunday he occupied the usual seat: right side, fifth pew from the front, third person in. He came to hear his wife's preacher. "Putting in my time," he always said. Even now he smiled.

But suddenly there was pain in his chest, shortness of breath, no breath.

Then he had seen that great light—blinding, razing light, hurling its rays like boulders. And he'd heard the voice. It sounded awful, like a train slamming into a truck, recapping his life, the whole sordid mess.

He still wondered, *How had He known everything? Everything!*

Jeremiah had knelt before the voice, saying, "Your will be done," as if he had a choice. And then it was over. He had agreed. Justice was demanded and exacted.

But now his mind was filled with feathers on the wind. Each logical conclusion slipped away.

He found himself dropped—no, falling—somewhere. But where?

"When it brightens up a bit, I'll take a look around," he murmured. His voice had a whispery sound, as when you think something so clearly it sounds as if you've said it out loud, but you know you didn't.

Jeremiah strained his eyes, looked to his left and right. Nothing.

"Where am I?" he repeated, this time quite distinctly. But again, his voice vanished with an eerie, shadowy tone, and he didn't know whether he'd thought it or said it. He shivered.

"What is this nonsense?"

Ignoring his voice, he decided to begin to feel his way around. *I may be blind,* he thought. *Have to feel things. Maybe I've had an accident.*

He shoved his hand out into the darkness slowly. *You never know what you might strike if you do it too fast*, he thought. *Could hurt myself.*

Only moments before he had begged, screamed, to get out of that scorching light. Now. . . .

"God? Ha!" he cried. "I'm rid of You."

Moving around in the darkness, suddenly he trembled. His hand still seemed to be attached to him. He sensed its weight. But he found nothing to touch.

He reached for his nose. It felt numb, but he knew it was there. It began to itch.

"My nose itches!" he shouted. The same shadowy shout. He tore at his face with his hands. No relief. He scratched vigorously, yet the itching sensation lingered.

He stopped, cocked his head, and listened. *No sound near, far, or anywhere. No hum of traffic. No cricket chirps. No snoring, breathing.*

"What about my voice?" he said. "There must be sound to it," he said. He whispered, "I'm here, all safe and sound." He let the "s's" linger. But it seemed to disappear into the darkness, as though muffled in folds of cloth.

He shouted,"I'm here! I'm here! Where is everybody?"

No one answered. Not even an echo.

He felt himself sweating. Instinctively, he raised his hand to his brow. But that same awful sensation of impotence gnawed at him.

Beads of sweat slowly moved down his forehead, cheeks, and nose. Soon, his whole face prickled with hotness, wetness.

"A towel! I need a towel!"

No answer.

He bent down to feel madly along the bottom of wherever he was. But there was no floor.

No floor! I'm standing on nothing. "But how?" he screamed. "How?"

Anger flashed through his body. His belly tightened and a familiar pain struck his side; the perforated ulcer began to burn.

"I'll lie down," he said. "That always helped."

First he bent. Then he leaned. He was still upright. He curled into a ball and lunged—there was no up or down or sideways.

"What kind of trickery is this? Where am I?"

The darkness and silence gave no clue. All he had been able to remember was light—vicious, penetrating, razing light, raw and pure as liquid. No more than liquid. Fire. Fire that burned through you until you screamed to be taken away. All he had wanted at that moment was to get away.

Then there was that voice. High. Omnipotent. The words had flashed like lightning, each one belting him like a boxer's gloved fist.

Jeremiah had tried to run. For an endless moment, he was held in place. Finally, he was cast out.

"Cast out?" he mused.

A hollow yearning pulled at his belly. "I suppose the food in this place is as strange as everything else."

Where could I go to find out?

He moved about, perhaps for an hour, or what seemed like it. But nothing changed, except his now ravenous appetite.

His mouth felt drier each moment.

Why am I burning? How can I feel flames without their causing light? That desert was bright . . .

During the war, his platoon had run out of water. Jeremiah remembered the maddening thirst, lying on the sand and panting. Mercilessly, the sun had hammered his forehead. His body screamed for water. Every pore felt like fire.

And then they found the sea. It was all he could do to crawl. Others walked as he inched his way. They drank as he struggled on. And they died, their stomachs full of salt water. But he lay helpless, just like now.

Can't lie, can't eat, can't even scratch my nose.

Tears slid down his face. But as hard as he tried, he couldn't wipe them away. "Answer me! Who are you? Where am I? Answer me!"

The darkness still engulfed him, passive and silent.

Now he found himself soothing his conscience.

That's it. Just make yourself laugh. Then you'll snap out of this.

He began telling himself a joke.

But then another strange thing happened. He couldn't recall the punch line. The more he thought, the more agitated he became. He began going through the alphabet, trying each letter to see if the word began with it. He couldn't remember at all. The punchline was gone.

Then something else came to mind—sex. He tried to catch himself. *Don't think of it, or you'll be in the same fix you are now with the thirst and hunger.*

But it was all there in his mind. Instantly. The tension mounted. But he had no power to satisfy the craving. The desire only seemed to build. Still, no climax terminated the feelings. No edging back into peace and serenity grasped him.

At the same time, his body didn't even seem to exist!

Instantly, it struck him: "I don't even exist!" he yelled. That did make him laugh, a bitter, cold, chilling chuckle in the darkness.

In his youth, he often wrangled with the fanatics about life after death, the deity of Christ, the existence of God, and other *ludicrous subjects*, as he called them. He especially enjoyed trouncing them with his incessant logic. But one of his pet theories was non-existence. "When you die," he told them, "you're gone forever. Poof. Nothingness."

Now he groaned. *But how can I not exist? I feel everything, every desire.*

He waited, hoping for an answer. But none came.

"Do I exist?" he cried. "At least tell me that."

His desires and feelings of thirst and hunger began accumulating, piling up. Fears, dreams, lusts, the desire for ice cream, the thirst for a sip of whiskey, the desire to play a game—and win. But no satisfaction anywhere. He was an empty cavern with no end to the torrent pouring through.

"Is this hell?" he whimpered. "Is this hell?"

Then he started to laugh.

"Hell? What's that? There is no hell."

He paused. "And for that matter, there's no God."

But there had been the light, and that voice . . .

Jeremiah had bowed before Him, admitting to many deeds. Now it was all coming back.

Still, that couldn't have been God.

"It was a dream. A nightmare. It'll be over as soon as I wake up." But he wasn't sure.

"Is this hell?" he roared again, trying to lash out into the darkness, to send his voice as far as it would go.

"Is this hell?"

But the roar tore his throat. The sudden pain knocked him back and he grasped his neck, trying to calm himself. It felt torn, ripped. He could barely speak.

He coughed in the darkness, and fought to settle himself.

"Tell me," he rasped. "Tell me, please tell me, at least that! Just tell me, is there a God and is this hell? I've got to know. At least let me know that."

If I could just hear a voice or even feel a touch . . .

"I don't know where I am. I don't know why I'm here. I know absolutely nothing about this place and yet I'm gritting my teeth, weeping, and sweating . . ."

My throat is on fire. I thirst. I hunger. I lust. What is it? What is going on? What has happened?

Then he remembered the cold, harsh words of the voice. "Depart from Me, you who practice wickedness."

"Is that it?" The question died on his lips. "Have I been wrong all along? Am I really lost?"

It couldn't have been Him. Not Him. God? God Almighty?

"What about my profession of faith?" he yelled. "I walked the aisle and prayed the prayer. The preacher said I was a Christian now. Everyone was weeping and congratulating my wife."

He paused and waited. It occurred to him that he should be brutally honest about it. Maybe that was the key. "All right, I did it just to please my wife. But I still did everything they said."

He grew hopeful, as though he'd just discovered an ace in his pocket. "Ha!" he challenged, "what about all that? I did do everything they said."

He waited. He listened. His sense of expectation rose, the way you feel when you expect a phone call any minute.

He wrung his hands together. He strained towards the darkness. He turned his head expecting some acknowledgement.

"I suppose You won't even answer that," he said mockingly. "Well, I don't care. You've put me here and I'm going to curse You and hate You as long as I can."

"I curse Your name God, and Your 'wonderful' justice. I hate You and Your dirty little book and Your Son who died and all that. I'm going to hate You as long as I'm down here. Until you let me out, I'll hate You and loathe You. Hear that? You're nothing to me, God. Nothing. The major Nothing of the universe!"

Jeremiah paused for effect.

I'm screaming against my own air. I can't do anything to Him. Nothing.

He made yet another disturbing discovery. His hatred began to coil up within him, ready to spring. Burning malice and anger flooded his being, like in the old days when someone spoke to him "of his soul." Yet there was nowhere to direct his wrath, except within.

Terror gripped him. *It's impossible. Preposterous. But I can't end it.*

"Maybe it will end," he murmured. "Maybe it's just for a little while. Like purgatory." He'd heard of that. Laughed at it. But maybe this was where he was. Being purged.

But nothing was going out of him. Rather, everything twisted up inside of him and mounted. He wasn't being purged. He was being deluged, filled, readied to explode, yet not finding release.

Then something new hit him so fiercely it almost took his breath. "How long do I have to wait?" he cried. "How long? There has to be an end. All things end sooner or later. Please tell me. How long?"

Immediately, he remembered the voice, "Depart from Me!"

Had He said, "Forever"?

The blackness seemed so immense, and the silence was as vast as a cindered landscape.

How can it be? The silence is the worst. No one. No friend. No enemy. No one to talk to. No one to curse, or counsel, or tell off. No one. No where. Nothing.

"You've got to tell me that," he cried again. "How long does this last? Please say it. Anything. Ten years? A hundred? Even a million? Just let me know how long."

He remembered the Voice's words, how they echoed as he was carried out. "Forever! Forever! Forever!"

Jeremiah swallowed and closed his eyes. "No! It can't be! Not forever! Please, it has to be less than that. I can stand anything if I know how long. How long will this be? Tell me. Please have that much mercy!"

He fought back the tears. "I won't cry," he said. "I won't. I won't give them that." Instantly, he swung around. "No, please, I can't stand it. I didn't know it would be like this. Please. Have mercy. Please, have a little mercy."

The moment he said "mercy," a new revulsion came over him. *Mercy? Mercy! I never asked for mercy in my life, and I'm not starting now, not even here.*

Then he remembered what he'd said, to the Voice, to God. "Take Your mercy, God, and Your world, too. Take it all. I don't need it. I don't want You or Your mercy, or anything of yours. I just want to get out of here."

What had He said? "So be it. You have said so by your

own lips."

So be it.

No! It couldn't be. That couldn't be the end.

Jeremiah fought to push his thoughts away. But they were screaming inside him. *Just a drop of water! Just a piece of bread! Just a friend! Just someone to talk to! Please!*

He waited. Something had to happen.

But nothing did. It was as silent and burning as ever. Immediately, a rage flooded through him like the flames of a bonfire. "Take Your food and Your water and Your people and shove it, God! Shove it! I don't want any of it. Hear me? Do You hear me? I hate You! How do You like that? Do You feel it? Does it make You want to cry?"

He waited. But nothing changed. Only his desires, the raging thirst, and the burning in his belly seemed to increase.

"I can't get to Him," he moaned. "I can't touch Him."

He fought to think. What could he do? How could he get back at God? How could he hurt Him?

But then something even stranger happened. As his thoughts and anger became clearer, he realized the only way he could direct it was at himself. He could now hurt no one in existence but himself. Not his wife. Not his children. Not his boss. No one. No one anywhere.

He gasped and tried to loosen the tightening around his neck, the pain he always got when he was terrifically afraid. But the tightening only continued.

He twisted around, shaking his fist and gnashing his teeth.

Gnashing their teeth. Wasn't that what the Bible said?

The thought struck him deep. He was in hell. This was the end. This was his end. All those elaborate plans and he had come to this.

But I'll get out! I'll find some way! I've always found a way!

He waited. Still nothing changed. Only his jaw pained now and the tightening around his neck and the fire in his gut seemed to increase.

Suddenly, he screamed, "I hate you, God! Hear that! Take it all. I don't care how long it takes down here. I'll wait You out, God. Hear me? I'll wait longer than You. I'll beat You at Your own game, God!"

The darkness and silence only seemed heavier, darker, quieter.

God has condemned me forever. I'd thought it was all a weakling's religion, a bunch of nonsense.

He remembered all the services he had attended, all the times his pastor had spoken to him, all the times his wife had prayed and pleaded.

"Why didn't I believe?" he shouted. "Was I insane?"

His thoughts seemed to shout back: *Because you thought it was nonsense. Remember? Boring. A real pain you could live without. Remember?*

Jeremiah looked up, straining his neck. "Is there no hope?"

The unquenchable desires within him began another rampage. He smelled smoke, fire. "Brimstone," he murmured. "It's brimstone." It burned inside him, scorching his soul.

"That's where I am, aren't I? Aren't I, God?"

He thought back, through his life, everything he'd ever done. Nothing in life was like this. There had to be a way out. There had to be.

But the words came back to him. *Forever! Forever! FOREVER!*

He fought to think of some way out, some way beyond. There had always been that back on earth. Hope. For a better day. For a change. For something to give.

But here there was nothing but darkness, silence, and internal fire.

He fought against the feeling. No, he had to find hope, something that spoke inside him, that calmed his soul.

But deep inside he knew. He had even agreed with Him. The punishment was just. In fact, he had wanted it—to get back, to punish God, to hurt Him. But more—anything to get away from that light, that burning, searing Light.

"Forever?" he murmured. "Forever?!"

No, it can't be!

He shook his fist and snarled. The burning raged on.

"Is that it, God? Forever?"

He fought for control. He fought to hold back his feelings.

Suddenly, he shrieked, "Why didn't I believe? Why didn't I trust Him?"

He knew the answer. It coiled and burned and raged within him. *Because I hated Him and His rules and His people and His book. I hated everything about Him.*

And why?

There was no good reason! No good reason! He was good. He was just. He was kind. He offered me every opportunity. And I rejected Him. For no good reason. I just did.

As he thought it, something struggled deep within Jeremiah. *I've been a fool,* he thought. *A complete fool. I blew everything. And now I'm lost. Forever!*

He gasped. He closed his eyes and tried to think. But there was no more thinking. It was over.

Weakly, quietly it started. But it began to build. Higher, higher, stronger, tearing through his whole body, soul, and mind. His throat ripped and burned, his whole body shook, and his mind burned with pain and fire. Soon he could hear nothing else but the plaintive, broken wail of the damned.

A *Second* Destiny

It wasn't hard to remember anything. We met Him in the air, as it had been written. At the time, it had seemed impossible that such a prophecy could be fulfilled so exactly. But when it happened, everything became clear. In an instant. We all knew that this was as it had been written all along. Nothing had been left to chance, or misinterpretation.

But now we were to stand before Him. Somehow this moment, this day always seemed so distant, so far away. But there I was. All of us, gathered. White robes like light. Faces so beautiful and young. Everyone delighted, ebullient, secure.

But I was so afraid. What could He say about me?

All my life, I'd known the words. "He will repay everyone according to his deeds." "We must all stand before the judgment seat." "He will recompense us for our deeds in the body, according to what we have done, whether good or bad."

I always thought . . .

What does it matter what I had thought? This was reality. This was the real thing. There was no hiding now, no going back.

I knew very well what would happen, or, should I say, could happen. That passage in Corinthians—he shall escape "as through fire." That was me. I might as well not try to hide it. Everything would be burned up, nothing left worthy of reward.

What was a salesman? What was the machinery industry? What was being a husband and father? Anybody could do those things.

Of course I wished then I'd done something grand. Like some of those early fathers. The "Golden throated." Who was he? Chrysostom, yes. Or one of the great monks. Then there had been others: Pope Gregory, Augustine, Thomas Acquinas, Luther, Calvin, Zwingli. I had heard about them. Then Wesley, Whitefield, Spurgeon. Pastors I had sat under referred to them all the time.

Joan of Arc, Tyndale, Hus. It seemed as though history was dotted with them like great bolts of lightning emblazoned upon the pages of writ.

Next to them, who was I?

I tried not feeling sorry for myself. In fact, I couldn't. All I could feel was a vague sense of regret. At one time I had sensed a call, at least I thought I had. But circumstances had prevented . . .

No, I couldn't use that excuse.

Things had just never worked out the way I'd hoped. I had been afraid mainly, and young. Then middle-aged. Then old. Then too late.

I had tried to do things. But I hadn't been good at them. Teaching in the Sunday School, what was that? None of my students went on to be great pastors or teachers. Least none that I knew.

Serving on the deacon board? I had been asked several times. But I never felt qualified. Who was I? Just a salesman. Sometimes I knew I hedged. Sometimes I knew I had to do things I didn't like. I always confessed them and tried to make them right. But it never endeared me to the diaconate.

Still, maybe it all had been just an excuse. I figured now He'd bring it all up. I'd stand there and He'd fix me fiercely with those lightning eyes and point it out. "Why?"

Oh, that question. I was so afraid of that question.

Please understand. I'm not trying to make you feel sorry for me. I just didn't see what I'd amounted to. I had been a salesman mainly. I did decent work. I had tried to be honest. When I hedged, I always tried to make it right. I sold a good product: printing machinery. I advanced in my company. I gave people a fair shake.

But who didn't try to do that? It had little to do with being a Christian. I suppose in a way I'd done it just to make sure nothing came back on me. In that industry, things had a way of hitting you over the head a year or two down the road if you weren't straight with people. But there had been lots of men who had nothing to do with Jesus—and who, I suppose, were now consigned to hell—who had done the same. What did that merit? I certainly couldn't see anything.

I hadn't been anything but an average guy.

Man, I hated saying it. It sounded so stupid. "Pretty average guy." Maybe "less than average" was a better description.

At the time, I didn't know. I felt so wrung out about all of this. The end of earth. The last times. The beginning of the new kingdom. Now the judgment. I knew I was sounding rather sorry for myself, and I didn't like that at all. It wasn't not like me. But what was I supposed to say: "Hey, I can't wait till You make me Your right hand man, Lord"? I was not one of the disciples. I wasn't even a pastor. Or a missionary. I didn't even lead many people to Christ. I could count on my left hand the number of people that I know stuck with Him.

That bothered me a lot, too. I had tried. I had passed out tracts at times. I told people what I believed. I "witnessed," as we had called it in my age. But I never saw much fruit. Certainly not the "thirty-fold, sixty-fold, or a hundred-fold" that Jesus spoke about. I could remember one, maybe two folks. But I lost touch with them. I didn't even know where they ended up.

It was really horrible. I was beginning to feel worse and worse. Even with a new body and a sense of perfection, I felt a little sick. What was He going to say? What could He say? "Glad to have you here, Mr. Colter. Have a good eternity!"

I mean, how well could He sugarcoat a below average life?

Well, maybe it hadn't been below average. Maybe that was mock humility. I mean, I felt I had a good life. A decent life. I had enjoyed it. I liked things like church and worship and visiting people and trying to teach. I had even liked reading the Bible and praying. I wasn't any Holy Joe, but I did have something of a "spiritual walk," as we called it.

But in a way, I almost wished He could have simply passed over me. Like when the whole team won the trophy and no one was singled out for special mention. Or even if one was that was okay. So long as no one got special demention.

Is that a word? Oh, well, I was always coming up with new words.

But I knew everyone would have a chance to stand up. Each of us would stand on the Bema. If I could have sweated at that moment, I would have sodden my white robes.

What could He say? That was what bothered me. Even He'd have to stretch for it. And I knew He couldn't.

It was almost funny. Remember how back then we would try to "say something nice" about someone? I remember my father so many times saying, "If you don't have something good to say, don't say it." A lot of times, though, you'd exaggerate or make up something to make a friend feel good, even though you knew what you said was only half true.

He wouldn't do that. I knew it. He was holy, perfect, just. He couldn't make things up about me, or anyone else, just to make them feel good. That always has a bad kickback. Sooner or later you realize it was all just flattery and you lost respect. If there was one thing He did, it wouldn't be to cause me to lose respect for Him.

Anyway, it was over and done now. He'd have to stick to the facts, that was for sure. And what would He come up with?

I just didn't know. Frankly, I couldn't think of a thing. I had never gotten my name in the paper, except once as a Little League manager of my son's team. And I never wrote a book, or sang a solo, or preached a great sermon, or even discipled some super evangelist. The people I had discipled, well, they never did much better than me. They just lived, so far as I can tell, fairly decent, quiet lives with few to no big moments.

Anyway, what was the point of flagellating myself? I'd just have to take what came. Chin up, my Mom always said.

She was there, you know. I honestly hadn't thought she'd be here. But I was overjoyed. All those years of lambasting her with the gospel. And all along she'd believed. Not quite like me. But she had believed enough to satisfy Him.

Dad, too. And my sister and brother and members of their families. I had never thought it could be true. I had always been caught up in certain rather narrow interpretations of things. But they all had believed. They hadn't had the kind of "lightning bolt" born again experience I had. I'd always thought that meant they didn't really have the faith. But they did. I was glad. We'd already spent a lot of time crying and thanking the Lord about it.

Of course, my three kids were there, too. And my wife. I don't know what I would have done if they hadn't made it. But I had been confident they would, of course, because I knew they believed. Still, I hadn't personally led any of them to Him. That was what troubled me. I led, as I said, only a few to Him. I just hadn't been the evangelist type. That was my fault, I suppose. Maybe I should have tried harder.

But still, I was there now, and I'd have to stand up to what was said and done. Even if there was nothing remembered, even if He couldn't honestly say, "Well done," I was still there. There was plenty of rejoicing in that.

But I wished . . .

No, had to stop that. Whatever came came. I'd just have to find joy in His salvation.

Of course, that was the main issue. And I did find joy in it. I was there. I was part of His kingdom forever and ever. I could never be lost now. My loved ones were there. Most of them. And it would never end.

But I wished . . .

Then it began. He called us by name and each one came forward.

It was really quite astonishing. I wasn't been bored or tired for a moment. He stood each one before the rest of us. It was like we could see right into that person, his very heart was revealed. And we saw all that he or she had done. I was astonished. We went right on through the ages, right from the beginning of time.

There was no way to tell time. In fact, in this place there was no sense of time. You could concentrate completely on what happened around you without forgetting what went before or what was coming after. But I'm sure what took place took several years in earth time.

Still, there was no way to tell.

And it didn't matter. It was all very enthralling and interesting.

I was looking forward to the twentieth century, though. I had some things to say about people I had known. In fact, I had already gotten opportunities about people all through history who had had a special ministry in my life. I got to thank Habakkuk and Elijah and Abraham, all of them. Paul, Peter, James. Everyone in the Bible at one time or another I had a chance to speak with.

It was quite marvelous, thanking and praising those people in person.

I was able to tell how reading things from various apostles and prophets had influenced me. I remarked on things I'd read from Martin Luther, and Calvin, and Wesley. All of them were rewarded. We all got a chance to speak and cheer.

Then He Himself spoke. So many "Well dones." So many accolades.

I almost wished I had been some of those people. They'd done so much. But I would be content, I knew, with whatever happened, even if it was very little. There were a few, yes, a very few, who seemed to "escape so as through fire." But even in their cases . . .

It choked me up to speak of it because I knew I might be one of them. So I didn't want to sound hard, or disappointed when it happened to me.

Still, it was all very exciting and uplifting. Each person was unique, and had made an important contribution. I just wished . . .

No, I had to stop saying that. Whatever happened to me happened.

Before He spoke, He gave the whole group a chance to tell and bear witness to what the present person on the judgment seat had done. It was all rather amazing, the things that were said. Words, kindnesses, good deeds, thanks, praise. It was all remembered. Some of them—like Paul and Peter, for example— the talk just went on and on until He Himself pronounced a judgment and gave the reward. Yet, so many received similar rewards to both Paul and Peter. I almost began to hope that He might find something about me. . . .

But I pushed the thought away. There was nothing to change. Nothing I could change. My life happened the way it happened. If He gave me a reward for anything, that was His business.

But still, I wanted, I hoped . . .

I knew I had to get off those thoughts, so I began concentrating on the proceedings again and not thinking about myself.

He took each of us by order of birth and gave everyone a chance to speak. Then He opened the book—their book, the one on each of their lives—passed it to them through the fire and whatever gold, silver, and precious stones were left, He gave to the subject as part of their reward. Then there were all sorts of crowns, and the hidden manna, the white stone, and so many other honors.

Each one was individual and complete. At the end, everyone agreed that His judgment was perfect.

Then He would speak. I tell you, it was a marvel what He said. I only hoped He had something good like that to say about me.

The moment I thought it, I pushed the thought away. It was a strange anxiety. On the one hand, I longed that everyone be rewarded so well. Yet, when it came to myself, the suspense was almost murderous. As though such a thing could be done in this place!

Frankly, I never wanted it to end. Everyone was so excited and happy. It was so exhilarating. You just wanted the person up there to do well and to receive a just reward. You were pushing for everyone. Then when He did pronounce His judgment, you knew it was right and exact, and took everything in. I felt that I trusted Him. I knew He'd bring it all out right.

The thing that troubled me was whether He'd really have anything He could honestly speak about.

Then He came to my year, 1950.

It was all so terrifying and yet exhilarating. It was getting to be a blur, yet everyone's deeds and face were imprinted on my mind. When I met them personally I knew I'd remember everything and even praise them for it.

But it would be my turn soon. What would He say? What could He say? I was practically jumping in place. It felt like a schoolkid having to get his report card and not being sure whether he'd get an F or an A or something inbetween. Why was I so unsure of everything?

Then He spoke my name!

I wove my way through the crowd to the bema. He motioned to me to stand before Him. He was so august, so resplendent. Like light. There was a warmth before Him. Something that filled you and made you feel confident. Love. That was it. He loved me. I could feel His love holding me and strengthening me.

Then He asked the crowd if anyone wanted to speak. My son stood forward first.

"There are so many things, Lord."

"Tell them all," He said.

I was astonished. We had had some bitter times on earth.

But my son began. "I remember him playing with me, Lord. Piggyback rides. Singing songs in the car. Fun. He made life fun."

He recounted all sorts of deeds. I was amazed and grateful. These were the things he remembered.

My wife said she always loved how I held her at times in bed, even when I was tired and wanted to go to sleep. She spoke of how I gave her money to buy groceries and clothing with a smile and not resenting it. It seemed she went on and on. A lump formed in my throat, and I fought to control my tears.

There were others who told of how I had taught them in church, how a Bible story stuck in their mind and influenced them later in life. One boy said, "He told this story one time in Sunday School about Zaccheus giving his money back to the poor. And later in life it motivated me to help some homeless people."

My mouth dropped open. He remembered that? I didn't even remember that!

And there were others. Johnny Martin—how I'd taught him to throw a ball. And Bill Briggs, a fellow salesman—how I'd been patient in training him and how he'd come to Christ years after he left our company. Doris Liston—how my strong singing in church one Sunday had encouraged her.

It went on and on.

Most of the time I was in tears. I couldn't believe it.

There was a lady named Gracie Schwartz who was stopped by the road with a flat tire and I fixed it. I hadn't even known she was a Christian. I had even witnessed to her, sort of, but she was bitter at the time about problems in her marriage and didn't tell me. She said my words had reminded her of the need to walk with Jesus aright.

There was a boy, now a man, from my Little League team, Casey Szabo, who spoke of how I had encouraged him and gave him a Bible verse. Even though he wasn't a believer at the time, it had come into his mind years later when he did convert.

It seemed like it would never stop. Every impression, every word—there were thousands of them—stitched itself into my heart.

But then the Lord Himself put the book in the fire. And suddenly there was gold, and silver, and jewels. So many pieces I couldn't count them. Each one a remembrance of a deed, a word, a thought, a prayer. It was all remembered. Every one.

The time I'd prayed for a friend during a funeral.

The time I'd turned off a leaky faucet in the company bathroom because I thought the Lord would be pleased.

The time I talked in church about the need to give sacrificially.

I'd forgotten them all. They seemed so insignificant. But He said that anything done in His name would last. And it did.

Then He spoke. He reminded me of how I had practiced Biblical principles in my work. He recounted and went through nearly every day how I had refused to lie or cheat or steal. How I had been honest, worked hard, and gave a good day to my employer. I hadn't even thought it mattered.

He spoke of how I had worked to be a good husband, listening to my wife and changing, growing, and learning, responding to her needs. He pointed out how I had stuck by her even when there were problems that could have ended in divorce. He remembered how I had tried to teach the family the Bible and applied its principles. Even though He had not given me gifts in the area of teaching or speaking, He said I had tried and done well.

I hadn't even remembered most of it. At the time, my efforts had seemed to fall on deaf ears.

He reminded me of how I labored to be a good father. He brought out deeds of gentleness and patience that even my children didn't remember.

Every time I had prayed in the car for someone, He pointed the answer out, and sometimes people stood and thanked me for my deed.

He showed me the accounting books of my giving to organizations and the church. Missionaries, pastors, people all over the world stood—from Nigeria and China and Israel, places I knew little about and had never visited—and they praised me for my deeds to them even when neither they nor I had known anything about it.

It went on and on. He moved on through my life, picking out each episode of good, showing who had benefitted. There were people who had become Christians through the smallest particles of my influence—a kind word, a tract, a prayer in passing.

There were people that I'd prayed for while standing in Supermarket lines. They'd become Christians, sometimes years later. He had them all stand. They thanked me and acknowledged my help. It was all remembered.

He spoke of others who were simply touched by my presence. He showed how many people in the gathering were influenced by me and my family saying grace in restaurants. Many times, at the time, I had only been vaguely uneasy. But He demonstrated that some of those people were moved in the direction of faith by those little acts.

Then He had all the people stand who were in some way influenced by some little thing I had done, whether it was prayer for a missionary in Europe, or giving a few dollars to an organization in Los Angeles. All of it was connected.

I could not count the number of people who stood and

cheered and thanked me.

I could not stop feeling choked up. The things I had done, the little things I considered so small and unimportant, had had these farreaching effects?

Finally, after it was all done, He stood to speak. He said, "John, turn to look at Me."

I looked into His eyes. It was the most hallowed, cleansing, exhilarating moment of my life. As I looked at Him, I saw His heart. It was all revealed in that blinding moment. I saw who He was, how He had loved me. I knew then that my God had loved from all eternity and I had been in His heart before I was even conceived in my mother's womb. I knew that He would never leave me and had been with me through every experience of life. I knew that He had ordered every detail of my life to bring me to this moment of triumph. I saw that long ago He had planned every chance at a good deed in advance so that when I came to this moment there would be much to reward me for.

I knew it all in that instant.

And in that instant I loved Him as I had never loved Him.

Still, He spoke, His eyes shining and true. "John, you have done all that I planned. You have done many good works in My name. You have touched the lives of millions. Well done. You will sit with Me and rule with Me on My throne. I welcome you into the joy of your Father."

He embraced me and in that moment, all the fear and doubt fell away forever. Then He presented me to the gathering. "Welcome John Edwards into the eternal bliss and reward of His Lord."

The cheering never seemed to stop.

And it was only the beginning.

Epilogue

You have told many stories in this book, Father.

Stories illuminate the mind and heart and move the soul. I like telling stories.

What is the greatest story of all?

Our story. History. His story. All of it, from beginning to end. That is the story that will be told forever in eternity, the story of redemption. I never tire of telling it.

It's a wondrous story.

I'm happy you think so.

Where do we go from here, Father?

Everywhere.

You will always be with me? With us? With all of us who believe?

Always.

That's enough.

It better be.

A card to the end.

It's just that there isn't anything else worthy of mention.

I understand. It's been a good journey, Father.

For Me, as well. Go now and tell the world and let them know I am here, I am waiting for their first call.

Always?

Always.

I look forward to heaven, Father.

It will come sooner than you think.

Just the same, I hope it comes sooner.

So do I.

I love you, Father.

I love you, My son.

We're going to make it through, aren't we?

Yes, we are.

Nothing will stop us.

Nothing.

It is good.

It is very good.

Good night.

I'll see you in the morning.

Conversations With God the Father
Mark R. Littleton

Subtitled: *Encounters with the One True God.* If you are greatly interested in improving your fellowship with God and want to know what He is like, then this book will help by presenting answers to questions as God might answer them, while painting a powerful portrait of His personality.

(hardcover)   ISBN 0914984195   **$17.95**

God Is!
Mark R. Littleton

"Heart-Tugging" inspirational stories, quotes, and illustrations that will leave a powerful mental and emotional impact on the reader. Short and easy-to-read sketches, embracing the attributes of God, will inspire your spirit and brighten your day. Topics include, God Is Love, God Is Good, God Is Wise, and more.

(hardcover)   ISBN 0914984926   **$14.95**

God's Unexpected Blessings
Edited by Kathy Collard Miller

Learn to see the *unexpected blessings* in life. These individual essays describe experiences that seem negative on the surface but are something God has used for good in our lives or to benefit others. Witness God at work in our lives. Learn to trust God in action. Realize that we always have a choice to learn and benefit from these experiences by letting God prove His promise of turning all things for our good.

(hardcover)   ISBN 0914984071   **$18.95**

God's Abundance
Edited by Kathy Collard Miller

This day-by-day inspirational is a collection of thoughts by leading Christian writers such as Patsy Clairmont, Jill Briscoe, Liz Curtis Higgs, and Naomi Rhode. *God's Abundance* is based on God's Word for a simpler, yet more abundant life. Learn to make all aspects of your life—personal, business, financial, relationships, even housework a "spiritual abundance of simplicity."

(hardcover)   ISBN 0914984977   **$19.95**

Revelation—God's Word for the Biblically-Inept
Daymond R. Duck

Revelation—God's Word for the Biblically-Inept is the first in a new series designed to make understanding and learning the Bible as easy and fun as learning your ABC's. Reading the Bible is one thing, understanding it is another! This book breaks down the barrier of difficulty and helps take the Bible off the pedestal and into your hands.

(trade paper)   ISBN 0914984985   **$16.95**

Daniel—God's Word for the Biblically-Inept
Daymond R. Duck

Daniel is the second book in the *God's Word for the Biblically-Inept* series designed to make understanding and learning the Bible easy and fun. *Daniel* is a book of prophecy and the key to understanding the mysteries of the Tribulation and End-Time events. This book is broken down into bite-sized pieces, making it easy to comprehend and incorporate into your daily life.

(trade paper)   ISBN 0914984489   **$16.95**

Life's Never, Ever / Always, Always Book
Michael S. Utley

Two books in one! This REVERSIBLE, irresistible book of definitely true words of wisdom will guide you with truth, humor, and sound advice on all the things you should NEVER, EVER or ALWAYS, ALWAYS do such as: *Never Ever, Hold Your Mouth Open While Throwing Food In The Air To Feed Seagulls,* and *Always, Always, Leave A Night Light On When You Own A Black Lab For A Housepet.*

(trade paper)   ISBN 0914984292   **$9.95**

If I Only Knew . . . What Would Jesus Do?
Joan Hake Robie

In what direction are you walking? Is it in His direction? And what about what you're saying? Would He say it? *If I Only Knew. . .* is designed with timely questions, poignant answers, and Scripture. When confronted with a nasty situation—stop and think—*What Would Jesus Do?*

(trade paper)   ISBN 091498439X   **$9.95**

The Miracle of the Sacred Scroll
Johan Christian

In this poignant book, Johan Christian masterfully weaves historical and Biblical reality together with a touching fictional story to bring to life this marvelous work—a story that takes its main character, Simon of Cyrene, on a journey which transforms his life, and that of the reader, from one of despair and defeat to success and triumph!

(hardcover)   ISBN 091498473X   **$14.95**

God's Vitamin "C" for the Spirit
Kathy Collard Miller & D. Larry Miller

Subtitled: *"Tug-at-the-Heart" Stories to Fortify and Enrich Your Life*. Includes inspiring stories and anecdotes that emphasize Christian ideals and values by Barbara Johnson, Billy Graham, Nancy L. Dorner, and many other well-known Christian speakers and writers. Topics include: Love, Family Life, Faith and Trust, Prayer, and God's Guidance.

(trade paper)   ISBN 0914984837   **$12.95**

God's Chewable Vitamin "C" for the Spirit

Subtitled: *A Dose of God's Wisdom One Bite at a Time*. A collection of inspirational quotes and Scriptures by many of your favorite Christian speakers and writers. It will motivate your life and inspire your spirit.

(trade paper)   ISBN 0914984845   **$6.95**

God's Vitamin "C" for the Spirit of WOMEN
Kathy Collard Miller

Subtitled: *"Tug-at-the Heart" stories to Inspire and Delight Your Spirit*. A beautiful treasury of timeless stories, quotes and poetry designed by and for women. Well-known Christian women like Liz Curtis Higgs, Pasty Clairmont, Naomi Rhode, and Elisabeth Elliott share from their hearts on subjects like Marriage, Motherhood, Christian Living, Faith, and Friendship.

(trade paper)   ISBN 0914984934   **$12.95**

God's Chewable Vitamin "C" for the Spirit of MOMs

Subtitled: *A Dose of God's Insight, One Bite at a Time.* Delightful, Insightful, and Inspirational quotes combined with Scriptures that uplift and encourage women to succeed at the most important job in life—Motherhood.

(trade paper)   ISBN   0914984942   **$6.95**

God's Vitamin "C" for the Spirit of MEN
D. Larry Miller

Subtitled: *"Tug-at-the-Heart" Stories to Encourage and Strengthen Your Spirit.* This book is filled with unique and inspiring stories that men of all ages will immediately relate to. Well known Christian writers like Billy Graham, Luis Palau, Max Lucado, and Gary Smalley share stories on Godliness, Mentoring and Friendship, Integrity, Marriage, Grief, Faith, Trust, Success, Purity, Spiritual Life, Family, On the Job, Christian Living, and Ministry.

(trade paper)   ISBN 0914984810   **$12.95**

God's Chewable Vitamin "C" for the Spirit of DADs

Subtitled: *A Dose of Godly Character, One Bite at a Time.* Scriptures coupled with insightful quotes to inspire men through the changes of life.

(trade paper)   ISBN 0914984829   **$6.95**

God's Vitamin "C" for the Hurting Spirit
Kathy Collard Miller & D. Larry Miller

The latest in the best-selling *God's Vitamin "C" for the Spirit* series, this collection of real-life stories expresses the breadth and depth of God's love for us in our times of need. Rejuvenating and inspiring thoughts from some of the most-loved Christian writers such as Max Lucado, Cynthia Heald, Gary Smalley, and Barbara Johnson. Topics include Death, Divorce/Separation, Financial Loss, and Physical Illness.

(trade paper)   ISBN 0914984691   **$12.95**

A Woman's Guide To Spiritual Power
Nancy L. Dorner

Subtitled: *Through Scriptural Prayer.* Do your prayers seem to go "against a brick wall?" Does God sometimes seem far away or non-existent? If your answer is "Yes," you are not alone. Prayer must be the cornerstone of your relationship to God. "This book is a powerful tool for anyone who is serious about prayer and discipleship."—Florence Littauer

(trade paper)   ISBN 0914984470   **$9.95**

Parenting With Respect and Peacefulness
Louise A. Dietzel

Subtitled: *The Most Difficult Job in the World.* Parents who love and respect themselves parent with respect and peacefulness. Yet, parenting with respect is the most difficult job in the world. This book informs parents that respect and peace communicate love—creating an atmosphere for children to maximize their development as they feel loved, valued, and safe.

(trade paper)   ISBN 0914984667   **$10.95**

Baby Steps to Happiness
John Q. Baucom

Subtitled: *52 Inspiring Ways to Make Your Life Happy*. This unique 52-step approach will enable the reader to focus on small steps that bring practical and proven change. The author encourages the reader to take responsibility for the Happiness that only he can find. Chapter titles such as Have a Reason to Get Out of Bed, Deal with Your Feelings or Become Them, and Love To Win More Than You Hate to Lose give insight and encouragement on the road to happiness.

(trade paper)   ISBN 0914984861   **$12.95**

Little Baby Steps to Happiness
John Q. Baucom

Subtitled: *Inspiring Quotes and Affirmations to Make Your Life Happy*. Inspiring, witty, and insightful, this portable collection of quotes and affirmations from Baby Steps to Happiness will encourage Happiness one little footstep at a time. This book is the perfect personal "cheerleader."

(trade paper)   ISBN 091498487X   **$6.95**

Beyond The River
Gilbert Morris & Bobby Funderburk

Book One in *The Far Fields* series is a futuristic novel that carries the New Age and "politically correct" doctrines of America to their logical and alarming conclusions. In the mode of *Brave New World* and *1984, Beyond The River* presents a world where government has replaced the family and morality has become an unknown concept.

(trade paper)   ISBN 0914984519   **$8.95**

The Remnant
Gilbert Morris

How far will the New Age philosophy with it's "politically correct" doctrine take us? *The Remnant*, the second futuristic novel in *The Far Fields* series, continues the story which began in *Beyond the River*—that of a world where a total authoritarian government has replaced family and rewritten history.

(trade paper)   ISBN 0914984918   **$8.95**

Baby Steps to Success
Vince Lombardi Jr. & John Q. Baucom

Subtitled: *52 Vince Lombardi-Inspired Ways to Make Your Life Successful.* Vince Lombardi is one of the most quoted success stories in the history of the world. From corporate boardrooms to athletic locker rooms, his wisdom is studied, read, and posted on walls. The same skills that Coach Lombardi used to turn the Green Bay Packers from cellar dwellers to world champions is now available to you in *Baby Steps To Success*. This book can help you be more successful in your career, personal, or family life. The same principles that made the Packers Super Bowl champions can make you a "Super Bowl" employee, parent, or spouse. These principles are broken down into 52 unique and achievable "Baby Steps."

(trade paper) ISBN 0914984950   **$12.95**

Little Baby Steps to Success
Vince Lombardi Jr. & John Q. Baucom

Subtitled: *Vince Lombardi-Inspired Motivational Wisdom & Insight to Make Your Life Successful.* Motivational, inspiring, and filled with insight that will get you off the bench and into the game of success, this wisdom-filled, pocket-sized collection of the best of Lombardi will help you one small step at a time to reach the goals you have imagined.

(trade paper)   ISBN 0914984969   **$6.95**

Purchasing Information:
www.starburstpublishers.com

Books are available from your favorite bookstore, either from current stock or special order. To assist bookstore in locating your selection be sure to give title, author, and ISBN #. If unable to purchase from the bookstore you may order direct from STARBURST PUBLISHERS. When ordering enclose full payment plus $3.00 for shipping and handling ($4.00 if Canada or overseas). Payment in U.S. Funds only. Please allow two to three weeks minimum (longer overseas) for delivery. Make checks payable to and mail to: STARBURST PUBLISHERS, P.O. Box 4123, LANCASTER, PA 17604. Credit card orders may also be placed by calling 1-800-441-1456 (credit card orders only), Mon-Fri, 8:30 a.m.—5:30 p.m. Eastern Standard Time. Prices subject to change without notice. Catalog available for a 9 x 12 self addressed envelope with 4 first-class stamps.   4-98